Ref – Lending
19/2020

FCS

Please return/renew this item by the
last date shown to avoid a charge.
Books may also be renewed by phone
and Internet. May not be renewed if
required by another reader.

BARNET
LONDON BOROUGH

K124

THE YOUNG OXFORD HISTORY OF
BRITAIN & IRELAND

Empire and Industry

1700 ~ 1900

Ian Dawson

General Editor
PROFESSOR KENNETH O. MORGAN

OXFORD
UNIVERSITY PRESS

OXFORD
UNIVERSITY PRESS

Great Clarendon Street, Oxford OX2 6DP

Oxford University Press is a department of the University of Oxford.
It furthers the University's objective of excellence in research, scholarship,
and education by publishing worldwide in

Oxford New York

Athens Auckland Bangkok Bogotá Buenos Aires
Cape Town Chennai Dar es Salaam Delhi Florence Hong Kong Istanbul
Karachi Kolkata Kuala Lumpur Madrid Melbourne Mexico City Mumbai
Nairobi Paris São Paulo Shanghai Singapore Taipei Tokyo Toronto Warsaw

with associated companies in Berlin Ibadan

Oxford is a registered trade mark of Oxford University Press
in the UK and in certain other countries

Text copyright © Ian Dawson 2001
Illustrations copyright © Oxford University Press 2001

The moral rights of the author/artist have been asserted
Database right Oxford University Press (maker)

First published 2001
Some material in this book was previously published in
The Young Oxford History of Britain & Ireland 1996

British Library Cataloguing in Publication Data available

Paperback ISBN 0–19–910831–5

1 3 5 7 9 10 8 6 4 2

Designed by Richard Morris, Stonesfield Design
Printed in Malaysia

CONTENTS

—— ❖ ——

CHAPTER 1

Trade and the first empire

❖

In 1719, book lovers first thrilled to the exploits of a young hero called *Robinson Crusoe*. Crusoe's exciting adventures on a desert island made Daniel Defoe's story successful, but so too did the believable setting. Crusoe was shipwrecked while on a voyage to buy slaves and Defoe's readers knew that there were many young British merchants, like their hero, who were trading in slaves, tobacco and sugar with European colonies in the Americas. They were making Britain more prosperous but they were also provoking quarrels with Spain, Portugal and especially with France over their empires. Defoe had not just written a great adventure story, he had seen into the future. Empire, trade and naval power were to dominate Britain's history for the next two hundred years.

An engraving of Liverpool published in 1779. Nowhere was Britain's wealth more evident than in her great Atlantic sea-ports. Between 1700 and 1780 the population of Liverpool grew from 5000 to 40,000. Defoe called Liverpool one of 'the wonders of Britain ... no town in England, London excepted, can equal Liverpool for the fineness of the streets and the beauty of the buildings ... and handsomely built as London itself'.

In 1702, 3300 merchant ships had brought £6 million worth of goods to Britain and exported goods worth £6.5 million. By 1770 there were 9400 ships, importing goods worth £13.2 million and exporting goods worth £14.3 million.

Slavery and empire

Since 1600 Britain's East India Company had traded from the Persian Gulf to the East Indies and particularly in India. The Company's merchants bought spices, cotton, silk, tea and opium for importing to Britain. However the new Atlantic trade from the ports of Glasgow, Bristol and Liverpool became far more valuable in the eighteenth century. Britain was adding to her colonies along the eastern seaboard of North America and among islands in the Caribbean, and taking part in the growing trade in sugar, tobacco – and slaves. Defoe described how Glasgow sent 'near fifty sail of ships every year to Virginia, New England and other English colonies in America'.

Trade with Asian countries meant that China tea, East Asian spices and Indian cotton cloth were sold all over Britain. In the middle of the century, for instance, a grocer in Kirby Stephen in Cumbria stocked ginger, cinnamon and quinine, as well as forty different kinds of cloth. Goods from China, and particularly porcelain like this bowl made especially for export, were called China ware. The term had spread to Britain from India in the seventeenth century; eventually it was used to describe all kinds of porcelain.

Of all the goods arriving in Britain, sugar from the 'West Indies' was king, making huge profits for the merchants and the owners of the sugar plantations, who used African people for slave labour. In 1690 the amount of sugar imported was 200,000 lbs. By 1760 this had increased to 5,000,000 lbs. Between 1680 and 1783 two million West Africans were carried in European ships across the Atlantic to colonies owned by Europeans. At first this trade in human beings was shared by Spain, Portugal, the Netherlands, France and Britain. However, by the 1780s two-thirds of the trade was in British-owned ships. The European slavers would land on the West African coast and buy their human cargoes from powerful African groups who had raided isolated inland villages and driven their prisoners away in coffles or chain gangs. The horror of the night raid and the march to the coast was followed by the terrors of the 'middle passage' on the sea, in which one in every ten slaves died, mostly from disease. One slave later wrote,

> The white people acted in such a savage manner and I had never seen such brutal cruelty. The shrieks of the women and the groans of the dying made it a scene of horror. One day ... two of my countrymen who were chained together, preferring death to a life of misery, jumped into the sea.

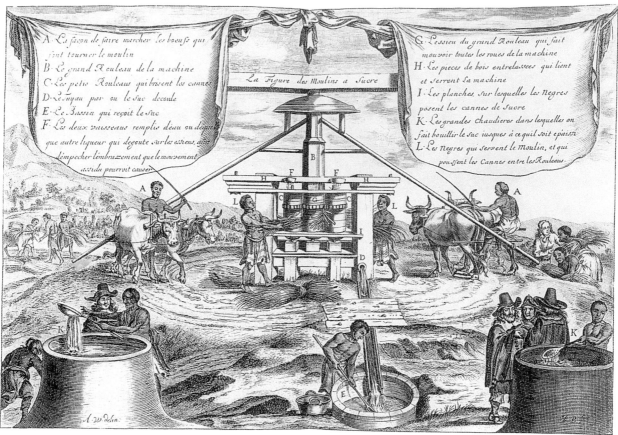

A French image of happy slaves drawn in 1681. In reality plantation owners spent little on shelter and food for their slaves, who were even beaten to death to warn newcomers not to rebel.

GAMBIA NEGROES.

TO BE SOLD,
On TUESDAY, the 7th of JUNE,
On board the SHIP
MENTOR,
Captain WILLIAM LYTTLETON,
Lying at MOTTE's wharf,

A Cargoe of 158 prime healthy young Negroes, just arrived in said ship from the river Gambia, after a passage of 35 days.
The Negroes from this part of the coast of Africa, are well acquainted with the cultivation of rice, and are naturally industrious.

CONDITIONS OF SALE.
To approved purchasers, bonds payable the first of January, 1786, and to those who make immediate payment in cash, rice, or any other produce, a proper discount will be made thereon.
ROBERT HAZLEHURST & Co.
No. 44. Bay.

During the eighteenth century it became increasingly fashionable for wealthy families to have black servants, bought as children from captains of slave ships. This was almost certainly how this page came to serve the family of Sir William Young, painted by Zoffany in about 1766.

Some managed to escape when they grew up, and join the free black population in Britain. Others had escaped from slavery in America during the War of Independence (see page 29) and joined the British army. When the war ended, many sailed to Britain with the rest of the army. By 1800 there were 20–30,000 free black people in Britain. Most of them lived in the ports.

Those who survived were sold to the plantation owners. Their treatment was exceedingly cruel. Some committed suicide or rebelled; others escaped and formed free bands, such as the maroons who held the inland mountains of Jamaica; many, many more died young. Between 1712 and 1768, 200,000 slaves were sold in Barbados but the island's population of black people increased by only 26,000.

Worldwide war

Every country tried to keep overseas trade in its own hands, believing that its own share could increase only at the expense of other leading European nations. Throughout the eighteenth century Britain won, by force, greater freedom to trade in the Spanish-speaking lands of South and Central America. France was Britain's most serious rival. She owned sugar-producing islands in the Caribbean which could also be used as naval bases. In North America, little of what we know as 'Canada' had been opened up to trade, but along the St Lawrence river and around the Great Lakes there was an important trade in animal furs. The fur traders' settlements were guarded by the great French fort of Louisburg on the coast. In India, the French East India Company made deals with Indian princes to keep the traders of the British East India Company out of their lands.

In 1756 the skirmishes between Britain and France burst into war, in the colonies in defence of trade, and in Europe in defence of Prussia. At first Britain lost territory, but when Pitt became Secretary of State for

The British victory at Plassey in 1757 opened the way for the East India Company to control Bengal, which was the sub-continent's richest province. This painting, by a British artist in 1760 shows Clive, leader of the Company's army, with the Nawab of Bengal.

War in 1757 he gave a new direction to his country's war aims: 'When trade is at stake you must defend it or perish'. He paid Prussia to stay in the war, and organized a series of hit-and-run raids on the French coast. This strategy left him free to concentrate the action of the British navy in the three key areas for trade. In India it took control of Calcutta. In West Africa it drove the French from important slave-trading bases, and in North America it forced them to surrender Louisburg.

The fall of Louisburg, in 1758, was soon followed by the greatest prize of all. The centre of French power in Canada was Quebec, standing on the Heights of Abraham which rise sheer out of the St Lawrence river. One British officer described it as 'one of the steepest precipices that can be conceived, being almost a perpendicular, and of an incredible height'.

James Wolfe, one of Pitt's hand-picked generals, led his men up that precipice at night in such secrecy that the French were quite unprepared. After a brief struggle, in which Wolfe himself was killed, the French army surrendered the city and with it French control of Canada.

The war ended in 1763, earning it the name of the Seven Years War. Britain had strengthened her control of North America, India and West Africa, and had added St Vincent, Grenada and Tobago to her clutch of sugar islands. She was even more clearly 'the most flourishing and opulent country in the world' which Defoe had described forty years earlier. Britain now owned enough overseas territory for later historians to describe the 1760s as the time of the 'first British empire'.

In his ship the Endeavour *Captain James Cook led a scientific expedition to the South Seas, with secret orders to explore the unmapped 'unknown southern continent'. In 1770 Cook landed in Australia (at Botany Bay), and claimed the land for Britain. On the same voyage he was the first to map New Zealand. In his later voyages he mapped much more of the Pacific Ocean. Cook's voyages were also remarkable for the health of his crews, who ate a varied diet and kept clean.*

Josiah Wedgwood, 'Vasemaker General to the Universe'

In 1759, the year of Wolfe's victory in Quebec, a manufacturer in Staffordshire, in the midlands of England, took over one of the hundreds of small workshops in the area already known as the Potteries. Since the 1730s Staffordshire pottery had been sold not only locally but also in London and even in Europe. This new manufacturer, Josiah Wedgwood, organized his workers in a different way from others. He used 'mass production' techniques. Each worker carried out one limited task which they could do almost mechanically. In the search for speed and high quality there was no room for individual creativity or for one pot being different from another; the aim was to make 'such machines of the men as cannot err'. This was the secret of his success. The results were beautiful and much in demand.

Josiah Wedgwood, the pottery manufacturer, and his family, painted by George Stubbs in 1780. One of Wedgwood's vases is displayed on the table near his elbow. Wedgwood took as much care over salesmanship as manufacturing. He opened showrooms in London and Bath, where 'sets of vases should decorate the walls and ... every few days be so altered, reversed and transformed as to render the whole a new scene'. He was the first potter to produce an illustrated catalogue, all goods were sent free of charge to the purchaser and they were 'at liberty to return the whole, or any part of the goods they order ... if they do not find them agreeable to their wishes'.

One of Wedgwood's beautiful Jasper vases, made in about 1787.

Wedgwood sold his most elaborate China ware to queens and dukes, but it was in the homes of the 'middling sort of people' that his factory products had the greatest impact. Since the days of Elizabeth I they had eaten off pewter. Wedgwood's Queensware, his cream-coloured china, changed all that. His identical, mass-produced dishes and plates could be stacked safely. His teapots poured accurately. They looked clean, could easily be washed and broken pieces could be replaced.

In 1768 Wedgwood confided to his partner, Thomas Bentley, his ambition to become 'Vasemaker General to the Universe'. By the end of the century Wedgwood's wares were bound for America, and others were presented to the emperor of China. In 1797 a Frenchman remarked that,'in travelling from Paris to St Petersburg, from Amsterdam to the farthest part of Sweden, from Dunkirk to the southern extremity of France, one is served at every inn from English earthenware'.

Turnpike roads and 'canal-mania'

All Wedgwood's ideas for new production methods would have been of little value if he had not found new ways to transport his raw materials to the factory, and his finished dishes to home and overseas merchants. Before the 1750s parish officials were responsible for repairing the roads but, as one traveller wrote angrily in 1752, the local labourers,

do not know how to lay a foundation, nor to make the proper slopes and drains. They pour a heap of loose, huge stones into a swampy hole which makes the best of their way to the centre of the earth. They might as well expect that a musket ball would stick on the surface of custard.

Road transport for heavy goods was difficult and expensive. Many manufacturers entrusted their goods to strings of pack-horses, thirty or forty strong, or even to 'poor crate-men who carry them on their backs all over the country'.

Wedgwood and other potters set up a turnpike trust to link well-kept roads with the main routes to London and Liverpool. The turnpike roads did speed up passenger and mail services but they could not transport heavy raw materials, such as clay. These were sent along navigable rivers in broad-bottomed boats. No such river reached the Potteries.

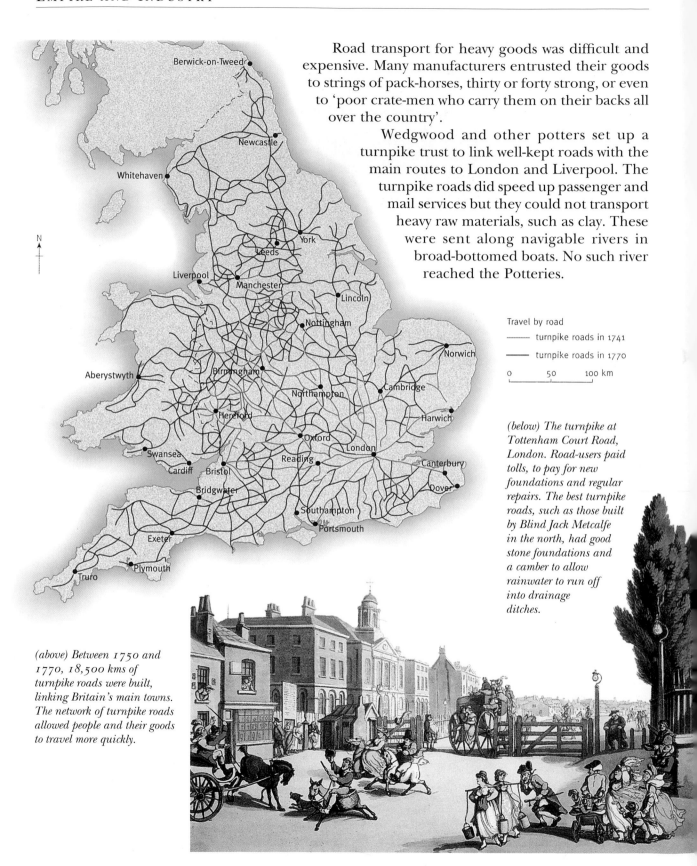

Travel by road
—— turnpike roads in 1741
—— turnpike roads in 1770

0   50   100 km

(below) The turnpike at Tottenham Court Road, London. Road-users paid tolls, to pay for new foundations and regular repairs. The best turnpike roads, such as those built by Blind Jack Metcalfe in the north, had good stone foundations and a camber to allow rainwater to run off into drainage ditches.

(above) Between 1750 and 1770, 18,500 kms of turnpike roads were built, linking Britain's main towns. The network of turnpike roads allowed people and their goods to travel more quickly.

Josiah Wedgwood's factory was rebuilt on the banks of the Grand Trunk Canal. By the 1790s he could send his goods directly by water to Liverpool, London, Hull and Bristol. Canals still depended on horses to pull the barges but, whereas a pack horse carried one-eighth of a tonne, a horse towing a barge could pull 50 tonnes of goods. Among the cargoes carried on the national network of canals was slate from Wales and Cumberland, which in many districts replaced thatched roofs .

During the eighteenth century the old unsprung coaches were replaced by faster stagecoaches, which often carried the mail as well as passengers. In 1700 it took over ten days to travel from London to Edinburgh, by 1750 it took six days, and by 1800 less than three. There were also many more coaches. In 1740 only one passenger coach went each day from London to Birmingham. By 1763 there were thirty.

One evening in 1765 Wedgwood gave dinner to James Brindley, who although nearly illiterate had planned and supervised work on Britain's first modern canal for the Duke of Bridgewater. This canal ran from the duke's Lancashire coal mines into Manchester and was so successful that the cost of the duke's coal in Manchester was halved; sales soared and his profits increased. Wedgwood asked Brindley to build a canal linking the navigable parts of the Trent and Mersey rivers. It was to be the Grand Trunk Canal.

It took Brindley's sub-contractors and their gangs eleven years to build the 240 kilometre Grand Trunk Canal with its seventy-five locks, but the canal cut the cost of taking Cornish clay via Liverpool and the Mersey to Wedgwood's factory by eighty per cent. In the opposite direction, Queensware could be transported to London and other southern markets by canal, river and sea, until in 1805 the Grand Junction Canal linked the midlands with the Thames, making the whole journey possible by canal. The increased profits were worth the many days when Wedgwood lamented that he thought of scarcely 'anything at all but Pottmakeing and Navigateing'.

Improving the land

'Both public and private wealth can arise from only three sources, agriculture, manufactures and commerce', wrote Arthur Young in 1770. 'Agriculture much exceeds both the others ... increasing general wealth and raising the income of all the ranks of the people'. Young, who was born in 1741 and died in 1820, spent his adult life writing about agricultural 'improvements', based on his tours around the farmlands of

Robert Bakewell called his sheep a 'machine for turning grass into mutton'. When Arthur Young visited 'the enterprising Mr Bakewell' he was shocked by the sight of 'some beasts ... so exceedingly fat as to be monstrous to the eye'. This painting is of Mr Healey's sheep. Healey, Bakewell and other breeders produced animals that both had more meat and could be fattened more quickly for market. Careful breeding led to heavier beasts for the meat market as well as bigger fleeces for the wool manufacturers.

In 1710 beef cattle at Smithfield averaged 168 kilograms; by 1795 it was a huge 363 kilograms. An average sheep in 1710 weighed 12.7 kilograms and in 1795 36.3 kilograms.

Britain, Ireland and Europe. He corresponded with farmers from Russia to the American colonies, where one plantation owner, George Washington (see page 30), built a barn according to Young's advice and sent to him for cabbages, turnips and seeds.

Young was right about agriculture. During the eighteenth century there was such a rapid improvement in crop yields and the quality of animals sent to market that historians have called it an 'Agricultural Revolution'.

At the heart of improvement was 'enclosure'. Instead of sharing in the common land (where villagers' animals mingled and shared diseases) and the strips of the open fields, each farmer had his own farm with fields enclosed by hedges. Enclosures had been taking place since the sixteenth century, but mostly in the sheep and cattle districts of northern England, Wales and Scotland.

The richest lands for arable (crop-growing) farming in the English midlands kept their medieval open fields until the 1760s. Then in twenty years they virtually disappeared, as rich farmers eager for greater profits applied to Parliament for the right to enclose the land. No longer needing to consult the owner of each strip of land, they introduced new crop rotations, manures and crops, such as turnips, which fed the animals through the winter. Between 1700 and 1800 the yield from each acre increased by forty-four per cent.

Young captured the essence of this revolution and his own excitement when, in 1768, he wrote about Norfolk,

> All the country from Holkham to Houghton was a wild sheepwalk before the spirit of improvement seized the inhabitants, and this glorious spirit has wrought amazing effects: for instead of boundless wilds and uncultivated wastes ... the country is all cut into enclosures ... richly manured, well peopled, and yielding a hundred times the produce than it did in its former state.

There were enthusiasts for improvement in every county and each had its shows and societies. In Wales the Breconshire Society gave away free turnip seeds and paid a travelling instructor to visit farmers. In Hafod, in Cardiganshire, Thomas Johnes, a printer who also owned some land, relocated peasants in more comfortable cottages and used his own printing press to print the reports of the Husbandry Society. In Ireland, Owen Wynne in County Sligo produced an improved plough while Henry Alexander of County Donegal reclaimed 300 acres or more, 'for the purpose of increasing his supply of manure'.

However, the improvers were still outnumbered by traditionalists. In 1773 Andrew Wight, a Scottish progressive farmer, complained that, the bulk of our farmers are creeping in the beaten path of miserable husbandry, without knowing better or even wishing to know better ... it is vain to expect improvement from them unless some public-spirited gentleman would take the lead.

Unfortunately, as Young pointed out, many 'graziers are too apt to attend to their claret [wine] as much as their bullocks'. Other farmers, interested in improvement, were hindered by lack of capital or lack of literature written in Welsh or Gaelic. The 'Agricultural Revolution' was neither as widespread nor as rapid as it sometimes seems.

Nevertheless the improvements in many areas meant that Britain could feed her rapidly growing population and, until the 1790s, even export grain. The 30,000 Welsh cattle and sheep which lowed and bleated their way along the drovers' roads to markets in England were heavier and meatier. So too were the thousands of black Highland cattle driven south and the countless geese which waddled to market, many wearing leather thongs to protect their feet. This increase in food was produced without an increase in the number of farm workers. Enclosure meant that cottagers were cut off from free supplies of firewood in common woods and grazing on the common land. Those who owned only a few strips in the open fields were not rich enough to pay their share of a village's Parliamentary Enclosure Act. They sold their land to take paid work as labourers on the larger farms, or joined the steady trickle of young men and women leaving the countryside to become the labour force in the new industries or on the new roads and canals.

Enclosures changed the appearance of the countryside, creating the patchwork of small fields divided by hedgerows shown in this landscape painted by John Constable in about 1810. Constable was becoming one of Britain's leading landscape painters.

The manufacturing revolution

When Daniel Defoe toured Britain in the years before 1720 he saw many bustling workshop trades. Sheffield was, 'dark and black, occasioned by the continued smoke of the forges making edged tools, knives, razors, axes etc and nails'. In Lithgow, in Scotland, 'the whole green, fronting the lough or lake, was cover'd with linnen-cloth, it being the bleaching season, and I believe, a thousand women and children, and not less, tending and managing the bleaching business'. In Newcastle, 'there were prodigious heaps, I might say mountains, of coal' and two industries which depended on it: glass making and salt distilling.

These were among the country's busiest districts, sending their products all over the country and into the wider world, but their manufacturing went on in small workshops or cottages, and it was often combined with farming. Human muscle, not coal or steam, still provided the power. Coal was mainly used to provide heat for glass makers, salt refiners and brewers. Steam was used to work pumping engines but not to drive machinery.

Fifty years later, in the 1770s, the numbers of people at work and the volume of goods they made in these manufacturing districts had grown dramatically. Glasgow's manufacture, which included linen, muslin and distilling, and its trade in tobacco, had made the city so rich that its population had grown from 13,000 in 1700 to 43,000 by 1780. In the textile industry in Lancashire, a series of newly-invented machines allowed handworkers to work more quickly and produce more goods: the flying shuttle for weavers, jennies and mules for spinners, and a stocking frame for hosiers. These new machines, worked at first by hand and then by steam from water-power (see page 44), used cheap imported cotton instead of linen. The stocking and hosiery trade in the midlands, whose main material had been silk or wool, also used cotton. This destroyed the trade in imported cloth from India and introduced the British to clothing which could be washed easily and replaced more cheaply.

In 1750 cotton clothes were luxuries, providing less than five per cent of Britain's exports, yet in 1785 an observer remarked,

> cotton yarn is cheaper than linen yarn, and cotton goods are very much used in place of ... expensive fabrics of flax; and they have almost totally superseded the silks. Women of all ranks from the highest to the lowest, are clothed in British manufactures of cotton ... they stand the washing as well as to appear fresh and new every time they are washed.

There was also a growing overseas trade for these British-made goods. Iron and brass goods

Cromford Mill by moonlight, *painted by Joseph Wright of Derby, probably in 1783. Wright was one of a group of artists who were fascinated by the effects of the new manufacturing industries on the landscape.*

Cromford Mill was built by Richard Arkwright in 1771 on the bank of the river Derwent. Arkwright used water-power to drive his textile machinery. His new factory was widely admired: 'We all looked up to him and imitated his mode of building', said the Lancashire textile manufacturer, Robert Peel.

This illustration of the iron works at Coalbrookdale comes from a book published in 1805 called Picturesque Scenery of England and Wales *by Philipe de Loutherberg. The chimneys, pouring out red smoke from the blast furnaces, are lit up by the glare from the molten metal behind. The man on the horse draws a sledge between iron castings beside the road.*

In 1776 Arthur Young described this as 'a very romantic spot, it is a winding glen between two immense hills ... too beautiful to be much in unison with that variety of horrors art has spread at the bottom; the noise of the forges, mills etc., with all their vast machinery, the flames bursting from the furnaces with the burning of the coal and smoak of the lime kilns'.

were exchanged in West Africa for slaves, and in Jamaica the slaves and their white owners used tools and wore clothes made in Britain

The changes in the textile industry were matched in other industries. In Birmingham manufacturers were making small metal objects (known as toys), buckles, buttons and other ornaments. To the west of Birmingham, at Coalbrookdale on the banks of the river Severn in Shropshire, the firm started by Abraham Darby was distributing its cast-iron goods, cooking-pots, firegrates and fire-backs by river, and later by canal. Coalbrookdale became the site of the world's first iron bridge.

The large-scale production of cast-iron goods dated back to about 1709, when the first Abraham Darby moved to Coalbrookdale and experimented with using coal instead of charcoal to heat his blast-furnace, to smelt the iron out of the ore. The first trials produced poor quality, brittle iron because the tar and carbon from the coal spoiled the iron. He succeeded when he tried cooking the coal into cinders before using it. This process gave him coke, which provided the same heat but without tar and carbon, and so produced stronger iron.

In 1757 the Dean of Gloucester, Josiah Tucker, who was also an economist, wrote, 'Everyone hath a new invention of his own and is daily improving on the work of others'. This search for new inventions was driven by the growth in household spending. By 1770, it has been reckoned, each family was spending over £25 a year on British-made goods compared with about £10 in 1688. In 1776 the Scottish economist,

Adam Smith, gave one reason why the extra goods were available: 'Good roads, canals and navigable rivers are the greatest of all improvements as by means of water-carriage, a more extensive market is opened to every sort of industry'.

Perhaps equally important was the steady growth in Britain's population. By 1770 it was perhaps 8 million, compared with about 5.5 million in 1700. Although many of the extra numbers were poor country folk with nothing to spend on new products, there was also a growth in the numbers of families of 'the middling sort'. A Derbyshire man, Jedediah Strutt, who made a fortune from cotton stockings, wrote about a day in London in his diary for 1767,

I was this day through Cheapside and could not help immediately reflecting that the sole cause of that vast concourse of people, of the hurry and bustle they were in, and the eagerness that appeared in their countenances, was the getting of money.

Yet the miners, knife-makers and textile workers described by Defoe in 1720 might not have been greatly surprised by the changes in their trades by 1770. There were more workers, a greater specialization of tasks and more hand-powered machinery to speed up production. Goods were produced in greater quantities. But this was still an age of manufacturing – of work done by hand – and not yet in factories.

Many British people recognized and were proud of these changes in manufacturing and trade. The writer Horace Walpole wrote to a friend, 'You would not know your country ... You left it as a private island living upon its means. You would find it the capital of the World.'

Towns in Britain in 1700
● towns with over 20,000 people
● towns with over 7000 people

0   100   200 km

In 1700 the largest towns in Britain were those which had grown since medieval times, mostly in the rich agricultural counties in the midlands and the south of England. By 1790 the new manufacturing towns had changed the map of Britain (see page 49).

CHAPTER 2

A Hanoverian kingdom

❖

In October 1770 a parson from Somerset, James Woodforde, invited five friends to dinner. Afterwards, in his diary, he described with relish what they had eaten,

a dish of fine tench, that I caught out of my brother's pond ... ham and three fowls boiled, a plum pudding; a couple of duck roasted, a roasted neck of pork, a plum tart and an apple tart, pears, apples and nuts after dinner; white wine and red, beer and cider. Coffee and tea in the evening at six o'clock. Hashed fowl and duck and eggs and potatoes etc. for supper.

Parson Woodforde was one of the 'middling sort', the people whose social position lay between the few thousand landowners and great merchants, and the mass of people who ranged from craftworkers to servants and labourers. The middling sort, who numbered at the most twenty per cent of the population, lived comfortably on incomes of between £40 and £50 a year. They bought carpets, books, wallpaper and other comforts. Shops in country towns stocked new fashions in the 'height of taste not inferior to the shops in London'. Dozens of local newspapers carried 'puffs' or advertisements trying to convince the middling sort that they too could live like gentlefolk.

A fashionable lady of the 1790s, wearing a silk and woollen dress.

A city of only 3000 people in 1700, Bath's population grew to 35,000 inhabitants by 1800. Each season, from October until early June, the spa city attracted 12,000 visitors. It became one of the most fashionable places, where polite society came to see and be seen. Between 1720 and 1760 Bath was largely rebuilt and today it still has some of the most beautiful examples of Georgian architecture. This is Lansdowne Crescent in 1820. In the city's elegant streets, crescents and squares polite society walked and talked. The more elderly members were carried from place to place in sedan chairs.

The rise of the 'middling sort'

Among the middling sort were doctors, lawyers, milliners and carriage builders, shopkeepers and jewellers, tenant-farmers and parsons such as James Woodforde. By the 1770s they were enjoying lives often of greater comfort than those of many lesser landowners and country squires. Their taxes were low. Trade increased with each decade. They ate well in comfortable homes. They subscribed to the new libraries and Assembly Rooms, such as those in Leeds or York, where they met, danced and gossiped. Their increasingly comfortable way of life set them apart from wage earners, who were usually miserably housed.

A very different gathering of the middling sort was the Lunar Society which began in Birmingham in 1775. Its members met on nights of the full moon, so that they could avoid the potholes in the road. They gathered to discuss the latest ideas about science, education, economics and politics. They included Erasmus Darwin, inventor and doctor, Joseph Priestley, a chemist and discoverer of oxygen, who was well-known for his republican views, Matthew Boulton, 'the first manufacturer in England' according to Wedgwood, Boulton's partner, James Watt. Wedgwood, although not a member, kept in close touch with them. Other towns had similar literary and philosophical societies. In Wales such societies helped revive the Welsh language and culture, publishing old Welsh heroic stories and Welsh dictionaries. The Scottish university cities of Glasgow and Edinburgh were famed in Europe for scholars who led discussions of new ideas, especially those of the philosopher, David Hume and the economist, Adam Smith.

(left) The Pump Room, Bath, where visitors met to take the spa water, to dance, play cards and assess their marriage prospects.

(above) A grand fireworks display in 1749 in Green Park, London. The German composer, Handel, who had settled in Britain, wrote the music. Bach, Mozart and Haydn all toured Britain. Fashion in architecture and the arts was still dictated from Europe and a new publication, the Encyclopaedia Britannica, *lamented in 1773 that, despite Britain's trading power, 'English is less known in every foreign country, than any other language in Europe'.*

THE ENGLISH COUNTRY HOUSE

In 1738 a wealthy Englishman called Edwin Lascelles visited Italy. Like other young men of his class, he had been educated in Latin and Greek, and he was eager to see classical styles of building. Lascelles was delighted by all he saw and in 1753, when he inherited the family estates, he was determined to build a home in the classical style that would rival the great houses of the nobility: Chatsworth in Derbyshire, Blenheim in Oxfordshire and Castle Howard in North Yorkshire.

The new house was designed by John Carr of York, but in 1758 Lascelles met Robert Adam, a Scot who had just returned from Italy. Lascelles and Adam needed each other.

◀ *The Music Room designed by Robert Adam. 'We flatter ourselves', wrote Adam, 'we have been able to seize with some degree of success, the beautiful spirit of antiquity and transfuse it, with novelty and vanity, through all our numerous works'.*

Elaborate French porcelain, bought for the house from the families of French aristocrats executed or impoverished during the French Revolution of 1789.

Harewood House as it appears today. The Victorians made additions and alterations to the original house.

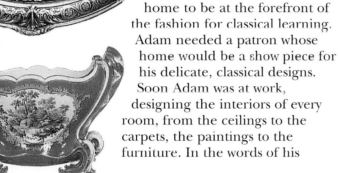

Lascelles wanted his new home to be at the forefront of the fashion for classical learning. Adam needed a patron whose home would be a show piece for his delicate, classical designs. Soon Adam was at work, designing the interiors of every room, from the ceilings to the carpets, the paintings to the furniture. In the words of his

A commode (chest) made by Thomas Chippendale which cost £86, twice the annual income of a comfortably-off doctor. Again Lascelles had chosen the most skilful craftsman. During the 1770s Chippendale designed furniture for thirty other country houses.

brother, Adam 'tickled it up so as to dazzle the eyes of the squire'.

When the house was complete, Lascelles turned his attention to the grounds, employing the most famous landscape designer in Britain, Lancelot 'Capability' Brown. Brown transformed fields and pastures into parklands and added plantations of trees, all designed to produce a natural rather than a man-made appearance. Harewood House lived up to Edwin Lascelles's hopes. It was one of the country houses pictured on Wedgwood's great dinner service for the Empress Catherine of Russia. In 1790 Edwin was created the first Baron Harewood. The Lascelles family had moved up into the ranks of the nobility.

Threats to the old order

Landed families such as the Lascelles believed that political affairs were their business and no one else's. The idea that other people should be consulted was hardly thought of. When the mass of the people wanted to express their views they had no other choice but to riot. People would riot, for example, if the local magistrates fixed new prices for bread, if laws controlling wages or prices were changed, or if a turnpike trust wanted to charge for the use of local roads. Riots usually began with some ceremony, like this one described by the *Gentleman's Magazine* in 1749,

> 400 Somersetshire people cut down a third time the turnpike gate on the Ashton road ... then afterwards destroyed the Dundry turnpike, and thence to Bedminster headed by two chiefs on horseback ... the rest were on foot, armed with rusty swords, pitchforks, axes, pistols, clubs.

The most notorious criminals were highwaymen, such as Dick Turpin who terrorized Essex until he was caught and hanged at York in 1739. Highwaymen even plagued the London parks where, according to the writer Horace Walpole, 'one is forced to travel, even at noon, as if one is going to battle'.

Leaders sometimes rode on horseback, carrying weapons (often rusty and useless) – an old tradition harking back to the idea that every freeborn Englishman had the right to bear arms to resist tyranny.

Rioting was not for the very poor. Their first concern was to stay alive. As London and other large cities grew, so did a class of people who could find none of the usual ways of earning a living: as a house servant, a craftworker or shopkeeper, a provider of street services such as carrying sedan chairs, carrying lights to lead people home, clearing piles of sewage or night soil. Henry Fielding was a London magistrate in the mid-eighteenth century, as well as the well-known author of the novel *Tom Jones*. He described how whole families had no food, warmth or shelter and that,

> oppressed with hunger, cold, nakedness and filth ... They starve and freeze and rot amongst themselves; but they beg and steal and rob amongst their betters ... There is not a street [in Westminster] which doth not swarm all day with beggars, and all night with thieves.

Poverty destroyed lives and health, and some became so desperate they abandoned their babies in the streets. In 1739 Thomas Coram opened a Foundling Hospital to take in these babies from London streets. Foundling Hospitals were opened in other towns, and in the later eighteenth century the first dispensaries gave medicine to the very poor and tried to cope when epidemic fever broke out. New private hospitals ran on subscriptions paid by the towns' wealthier citizens, which gave them the right to ensure that their own servants and the tradespeople who supplied them could be treated as patients.

The idle 'prentice executed at Tyburn, *engraved by William Hogarth in 1747. Hogarth was a leading artist working in the mid-eighteenth century. His pictures exposed the harsh living conditions of the poor and attacked the corruption of the government and the wealthy, but he also used his paintings and engravings to tell a moral tale. This scene shows the fate of a young man who fell into godlessness and vice. Another scene shows the other apprentice, Goodchild, who through hard work rose to be Lord Mayor of London. Executions continued to draw large crowds until 1868, when the government ordered that executions should take place inside prisons, not in public. By then criminals were no longer executed for theft, only for murder and treason.*

For the very poor, the only refuge was the workhouse. There, conditions were deliberately harsh to discourage vagrants (tramps and beggars) from wandering from parish to parish. Workhouses were stark, cold buildings where the homeless old and orphaned children worked at spinning and similar drudgery to earn their keep. Unscrupulous owners starved inmates to the point of death, and by the later eighteenth century, they were selling children to work in the new textile factories in the north of England (see page 47).

There was little mercy for criminals who were caught. Anyone stealing goods, worth only five shillings, risked hanging or transportation. Between 1717 and 1776, 30,000 criminals were transported to colonies in America and the West Indies to work on the plantations. Among them were many like nineteen-year-old Elizabeth Hardy from Norwich, who, in 1741, was sentenced to hang for stealing a few shillings' worth of goods, but her sentence was reduced to transportation. Yet, despite the public hangings, whippings and brandings, crime increased. The risk of being caught was not great, as there were still only a very few constables.

By the 1750s changes in manufacturing and trade had led a growing number of people to leave traditional agricultural labouring. They worked in clay, lead, tin or coal mines or in the new industries making pottery or cloth. Much of this manufacturing was piece work, done for harsh masters who paid low rates and took no interest in the lives of their workers. This was a change from the way the best squires, farmers and town householders had treated them. Many had seen it as their duty to help their workers and villagers in times of misfortune. Cut off from these traditional ways, workers in these new trades had little respect for the squire who might also be the magistrate, or the parson, who very probably came from a land-owning family. They stayed away from church and kept their children away from schools run by the clergy.

It was among the poor that the preaching of John Wesley found an eager audience. Wesley was an Anglican clergyman who, in 1738, was swept up by a powerful sense that he had been saved and could save others. He was joined by two others, his brother Charles and the preacher George Whitefield. Later Wesley wrote that, 'I felt my heart strangely warmed ... I felt I did trust in Christ, Christ alone for salvation ... and he had taken away my sins, even mine'.

That experience turned Wesley into an evangelist, determined to carry God's word to the people. Soon he was launched on his life's work of tireless preaching, often in the open air, to those neglected by the Church of England: Cornish miners, Stafford-shire potters, northern textile workers. He was not the first clergyman to spread the gospel by open-air preaching. In Wales, Howell Harris and others matched Wesley's energy. After hearing Harris, Charles Wesley wrote, 'Never man spake, in my hearing, as this man spake ... Such love, such power, such simplicity was irresistable. The lambs dropped down on all sides into their shepherd's arms'.

The leaders of the established Church of England were hostile to the evangelical preachers. The bishops wanted a polite, decent, orderly church. They refused to let Wesley preach in churches. By the time of his death in 1791, Wesley's open-air meetings had won over 70,000 converts and he had become the leader of this new Christian revival called Methodism, although he himself was always reluctant to be thought of as a rival to the Church of England.

John Wesley travelled over 400,000 kilometres to preach and lead prayer meetings. He was enthusiastic and impassioned and preached to groups who had no respect for the traditional Church. He gave these social outsiders hope, but the bishops in the Church of England feared he gave them 'exalted strains and notions', creating 'a disesteem of their superiors'. His meetings were sometimes attacked by mobs, stirred up by landowners who feared his ideas, but he refused to stop. He was greatly helped by his brother, Charles, who wrote over 6,500 hymns, including 'Hark, the Herald Angels Sing'.

God save the king!

John Byrom looked out of his window on to the deserted streets of Manchester. It was November 1745. A rebel army was approaching and many people had fled. In the silence Byrom heard footsteps draw near. Into view, he wrote later, came 'a serjeant and a drummer in a Highland dress, with a woman on horseback carrying a drum ... two men and a half taking our famous town of Manchester without any resistance or opposition'. By the next day Charles Edward Stuart's army of 5000 men had taken control of the town.

Charles, also known as the Young Pretender, had come to win back the throne which had been withheld, he believed, from his father James Edward, the 'Old Pretender', when Queen Anne died in 1714. In 1715 James had landed in Britain, expecting thousands to rally to the Stuart

Charles Edward Stuart, often known as Bonnie Prince Charlie. In 1715 his father, James Edward, had claimed the throne. He was the son of the Catholic James II who had been driven from the country in 1688. James Edward was also a Catholic. Parliament had instead chosen Queen Anne's closest Protestant relative, the Elector of the German state of Hanover, who became George I. The followers of James Edward (James is Jacobus in Latin) were called Jacobites and some became Jacobite rebels.

cause against the new Hanoverian king. Instead the Jacobites had been ignored by the British. He was defeated. Now, in 1745, his son was trying again.

Charles's early success gave him high hopes. At first he met little opposition, but in towns and counties merchants and landowners hastily recruited soldiers. Ballad writers tried out the words of a new patriotic song, which called on God to save the king and to confound the politics and knavish tricks of the king's enemies – the Jacobites.

The Jacobite army left Manchester and moved south but at Derby Charles stopped. For the first time he faced the truth. He now had only a few hundred English supporters. The royal armies were closing in. He turned and retreated. Even in Lowland Scotland he found few friends. The Act of Union in 1707 had shown Lowland merchants and farmers that they could gain from easier trade with the American colonies and England. To many Scots, Charles was not a national hero but a danger to their way of life and religion. In Glasgow, newly rich from manufacturing, Presbyterian clergy preached sermons loyal to King George even while Charles's Highlanders stalked the town.

In April 1746 the Duke of Cumberland's army caught up with Charles's exhausted forces at Culloden Moor, and defeated them. A large part of Cumberland's army was made up of Lowland Scots who were Protestant and loyal to the Hanoverian government. Charles fled to Skye and then to France.

The Battle of Culloden Moor, 1746. After the battle the Duke of Cumberland ordered the slaughter of all the prisoners and the wounded.

A short, fierce and bustling man, George II was the last British monarch to lead his troops into battle, at Dettingen in Germany when he was aged 60. He was often lazy in matters of government, which allowed devious politicians to hatch plots around him to gain influence.

Kings, Prime Ministers and Parliament

The Battle of Culloden ended the Jacobite threat to the House of Hanover. The first Hanoverians, George I (1714–1727) and George II (1727–1760), were not highly popular but they avoided making serious enemies among influential politicians. As kings, they still directed foreign policy and chose their ministers but learned to work with politicians. Both kings spent long periods in Hanover and gradually one minister began to have more authority than the others. This chief, or Prime Minister, began to take the lead in making government policy while the king was abroad.

The first Prime Minister was Robert Walpole, who dominated politics for twenty years between 1721 and 1742. He wanted to ensure that trade would flourish and this meant preventing war. His power depended on persuading the king and Parliament to support him. Walpole wrote that to influence the king he would act 'with tenderness and management ... the more you can make anything appear to be [the king's] own ... the better you will be heard'. Walpole managed Parliament by rewarding supporters with sinecures (well-paid jobs needing little work) and wooing others with promises of rewards.

By the 1740s it was accepted that the king, Prime Minister and Parliament worked in partnership. It was a matter of pride to men like Edwin Lascelles (see page 22) that the power of those families who owned most of the country could prevent the monarch or any of his favourite politicians gaining too much power. Even such powerful figures as Walpole and Pitt the Elder could not survive in office if they lost the confidence of Parliament.

From 1721 until 1742 Robert Walpole was the king's chief or Prime Minister. A short man who weighed twenty stone, he was blunt and outspoken. He played the role of a simple country squire, munching apples in the House of Commons, but lived amid splendour in Houghton Hall in Norfolk. In 1742 he lost power when Parliament demanded a vigorous war policy against Spain.

The strength of these leading families was visible in Parliament. The House of Lords was the meeting place for the noblemen but among the 550 or so MPs in the Commons there were also more than 100 sons of members of the Lords, together with 200 more who were from well-to-do landowning families. The remaining number of MPs was a mixture of merchants, lawyers and army and navy officers.

The House of Commons had to be re-elected every seven years, but the great landed families used elections to hold on to their influence in the House of Commons. Only one man in eight could vote. In boroughs (which were towns in theory but often far smaller) the franchise – or power to vote – went to the wealthy or to members of the borough corporation. However even they rarely had the opportunity to vote. Frequently no election took place because the borough was said to be 'in the pocket' of a landowner – all the electors were his tenants and they simply approved his chosen candidate. The Duke of Newcastle controlled up to twelve 'pocket boroughs' in England and Wales.

By the 1770s there was mounting criticism of this system. John Wilkes was the most notorious critic, supporting 'reform' to give the right to vote to even the 'meanest mechanic, the poorest peasant'. He believed that everyone should share in 'making those laws which deeply interest them, and to which they are expected to pay obedience'. There was also increasing criticism of George III (1760–1820), who began his reign determined to tilt the balance of power away from Parliament and back towards the monarch. These debates led to sharper rivalries among politicians, with the Whigs re-emerging as an opposition party, demanding reform and a clearer limit to royal power.

John Wilkes was known as one of the ugliest men in Britain, but also as one of the most entertaining talkers. 'It takes me only half an hour to talk away my face', he boasted. As an MP in the 1760s he led the demands for freedom of the press. He argued that newspapers should be free to criticize the king and his ministers, but when he did so in his own paper, The North Briton, he was arrested and expelled from the House of Commons.

The American War of Independence

In 1773 a fleet of British merchant ships sailed into Boston Harbour, Massachusetts in North America. Before the cargo could be unloaded, a group of Americans crept aboard, seized three hundred chests of tea and hurled them into the sea. This 'Boston Tea Party' was a protest against British taxes being imposed on the American colonies. The Seven Years War had ended in 1763 with the French leaving Canada. Some colonists said there was no need for them to pay to keep British forces in America, especially as they had no representatives in the Westminster Parliament, which voted for taxes the colonists had to pay. The colonists rallied round the slogan, 'No Taxation Without Representation'.

George III and his Prime Minister Lord North disagreed fiercely with the colonists. They believed the navy and army were needed to

Like many Americans George Washington was a reluctant rebel, who had fought alongside British forces against France in the Seven Years War. When he was appointed commander a fellow colonist described him as, 'discreet and virtuous, no harum scarum ranting, swearing fellow but sober, steady and calm'. His tactic was 'on all occasions avoid a general action'.

After the war Washington wanted to devote himself to his estates but again duty called him to help his country. He was elected the first president of the United States of America in 1789, insisting on being above party politics, taking no gifts and refusing hospitality. He was re-elected for a second term but refused a third, retiring in 1797.

protect British trading interests in North America, and insisted that the colonists had to obey the laws made in Westminster. The American colonies lay at the very heart of Britain's growing empire and trade. They took twenty per cent of Britain's exports and supplied a third of Britain's imports. Protests increased in 1764, when taxes on sugar were raised, and in 1765 when the new Stamp Act placed a tax on paper used for newspapers and all official documents. Finally the Boston Tea Party seemed to make war with Britain certain, although the first shots were not fired until April 1775.

The British were sure they would win. Britain was the most powerful country in the world, whereas the colonists' commander, George Washington, wrote,

> I should not be at all surprised at any disaster that may happen ... Could I have foreseen what I have, and am like to experience, no consideration upon Earth should have induced me to accept this command.

His men were short of food, clothing and weapons but Britain was slow to raise forces and this allowed the colonists to gain confidence. Once the war was underway the colonists had most of the advantages. It took up to six months to raise and transport British troops. Once there, the British Redcoats tried to fight in the way still used for pitched battles in Europe. Washington's tactic was to make use of his men's knowledge of the country to fight a guerrilla war, sniping, ambushing and destroying bridges.

With Britain in trouble, her European rivals turned on her. France attacked in the West Indies and India, Spain raided Florida and Gibraltar, the Dutch assaulted Ceylon and the East Indies. Britain had to withdraw troops from America to save her other colonies. In 1781 the task of fighting what seemed like the rest of the world proved too much. In North America General Cornwallis's British army was surrounded at Yorktown by French and American armies and the French navy. Cornwallis surrendered. The colonists had won their independence and the United States of America was born. The Declaration of Independence, issued by the colonists on 4 July 1776, was written by Thomas Jefferson. The Declaration became the basis for the American Constitution. Its most famous passage reads, 'We hold these truths to be self-evident, that all men are created equal, that they are endowed by their Creator with certain inalienable rights, that among these are life, liberty and the pursuit of happiness.'

A painting of the Irish House of Commons in 1780 by Francis Wheatley. Grattan is on the right of the table, arguing that the Irish Parliament, not Westminster, should be able to make the laws for Ireland. Even one of Grattan's opponents in 1782 said that his speech was 'splendid in point of eloquence ... No man presumed to call in question anything advanced by Grattan'.

The end of the British Empire?

The American colonists were not the only patriots fighting for freedom. In Ireland a patriot movement started among Protestants. Since 1688 they had dominated the country's political, social and cultural life, building up a Protestant 'ascendancy' in an island where Catholics made up eighty per cent of the population but owned only five per cent of the land. The Irish House of Commons in Dublin was made up entirely of Protestants, but the laws they passed had no force unless they received the approval of the Westminster Parliament. The patriots wanted to end this limit on their power to govern their own country.

In 1779, inspired by the success of the Americans, Protestant Volunteers demonstrated against English control, while in the Dublin Parliament Henry Grattan demanded an end to British control of Irish affairs. Lord North, fearing rebellion, persuaded the Westminster Parliament to give the Irish Commons some independence to make its own laws. 'Ireland', declared Grattan, 'is now a nation', believing that the Dublin Parliament could claim to rule a united Ireland. However, Grattan's 'nation' was still a Protestant one. The Westminster Parliament

An engraving illustrating the Gordon riots of 1780. For a whole week Londoners, including the middle-classes, rioted in support of Lord George Gordon, an unstable man with extreme anti-Catholic views. Property belonging to Catholics was attacked, so were prisons and the Bank of England. There were about three hundred deaths, mostly caused by soldiers. In Bath the novelist Fanny Burney noted 'the stage coaches from London are chalked over with "No Popery"'. The next day Bath's 'new Roman Catholic chapel ...[was] burning with a fury that is dreadful'.

had lifted restrictions on the rights of Catholics to own property and to enter careers such as medicine and the law, but Catholics still could not vote and Grattan's Parliament still excluded Catholics and Presbyterian dissenters.

Defeat in America and the set-backs in Ireland encouraged widespread opposition to the Prime Minister, Lord North and George III, who had argued that there should be no agreement with the American colonists. In Parliament an MP, John Dunning, proposed a resolution that 'the influence of the crown has increased, is increased and ought to be diminished'. Opponents of the government turned the pages of Edward Gibbon's *The Decline and Fall of the Roman Empire,* which had been published in 1776. Gibbon had written the best-known history book of the century, which described how the Roman Empire, supremely organized and powerful, had fallen apart. Some saw Britain in a similar position. Her empire had been much enlarged by conquest in the Seven Years War, but the American War of Independence had shown how difficult and expensive it might be to control and defend her new, far-flung conquests in the future. British mastery of world trade was in decline. Exports fell by twenty per cent between 1772 and 1780. Would Britain be able to hold on to her empire or was her growing wealth and power at risk?

CHAPTER 3

Victory over Napoleon

❖

The blame for the loss of the American colonies fell on George III and his Prime Minister, Lord North. North was forced to resign in 1782 and give way to the Whigs, but that only caused more problems. George still had the power to make and break governments, and he wanted to break the new Whig government as he resolutely opposed its ideas for political reform. At first George was only partly successful. He prevented the Whigs from forming a strong government, but he could not find a politician he trusted and who had enough support in Parliament to become Prime Minister. Eventually, in December 1783, George gambled by appointing William Pitt as Prime Minister. Pitt was the son of the William Pitt who had led Britain during the Seven Years War. He was just twenty-four years old. His opponents were outraged. They mocked the 'mince-pie administration' that would not survive the remaining week before Christmas, and they joked about a 'kingdom trusted to a schoolboy's care'.

George III, painted in about 1767. After the loss of the American colonies George III had less influence over his ministers, and he never controlled William Pitt in the same way as he had influenced Lord North. Between 1811 and 1820

George III's son, also called George, ruled in his father's place as 'Regent', as it was thought that George III was mentally ill. When he died in 1820 the Prince Regent became George IV (1820 – 1830) .

William Pitt addressing the House of Commons in 1793. William Pitt the Younger was always respected for his cleverness and hard work, but he was never popular. He was probably a very lonely man. The portrait painter Thomas Lawrence observed, 'all seemed to be impressed with an awe of him. At times it appeared like boys with their master'. He dominated politics throughout the French wars, dying when he was still Prime Minister in 1806, aged forty-six.

Prime Minister Pitt

Pitt's opponents were unable to gobble up his 'mince-pie' administration. In the House of Commons his debating skills won the votes of independent MPs. Behind the scenes George III persuaded peers from the House of Lords that only Pitt could save the country from chaos. By March 1784 the king and Pitt felt strong enough to fight a general election. His Whig opponents wanted sweeping changes and an end to royal influence. Pitt told voters that, after the disasters of the 1770s, the country needed stability with moderate reform and a partnership between monarchy and Parliament. Pitt was victorious.

Pitt was now secure as Prime Minister. Britain's trade began to recover. Exports to the United States of America increased in the 1790s, thanks to the constant American demand for ironware and other industrial goods. Pitt knew the country was prospering because people were paying more taxes on servants and luxury goods. He spent some of the increased revenues on building thirty-three new warships to protect colonies and merchants. Before the end of the 1790s the warships were needed to defend Britain herself from invasion, as events in France took a dangerous turn.

'Liberté, égalité, fraternité!'

In 1789 Arthur Young, the journalist and farmer, crossed the Channel to report on news of French farming. Instead he found himself noting how, 'the price of bread has prepared the populace everywhere for all sorts of violence ... the people will, from hunger, be driven to revolt'. In Strasbourg he watched soldiers and 'people so decently dressed that I regarded them with no small surprise', destroy the town hall. Young had ridden into the very beginnings of the French Revolution.

Paris was the centre of the revolution. The poor were outraged by high bread prices, unemployment and taxes which they paid but noblemen did not. In July 1789 the Paris mob stormed the Bastille, the prison which symbolized the tyranny of the king. Then, inspired by the example of the American colonists, their leaders declared that only their National Assembly, not the king and his court, had the power to rule France. They imprisoned Louis XVI and the revolutionaries' slogan *liberté, égalité, fraternité* became part of their published *Declaration of the Rights of Man and Citizen*, which declared,

> Men are born and remain free and equal in rights ... these rights are liberty, property, security and resistance to oppression ... every citizen may, therefore, speak, write and print freely.

Pitt greeted the news of revolution from France with caution. He refused to support the king or the revolutionaries, wanting to be on good terms with whoever emerged as the leader of France. His caution was drowned by the applause of radical enthusiasts, such as the members of the Lunar Society in Birmingham. Erasmus Darwin wrote to James Watt, hailing 'the dawn of universal liberty' and declaring, 'I feel myself becoming all French in chemistry and politics'. Wedgwood set about making souvenir medallions to celebrate the fall of the Bastille.

This enthusiasm spread rapidly. In nearly every major town skilled and literate craftworkers such as tailors, printers and metal workers formed political societies. The Sheffield Society for Constitutional Information was the first, in 1791. Members of the new London Corresponding Society read and circulated pamphlets about political issues. Their goal was to win the vote for all adult men. Their inspiration was the French Revolution, their 'bible' was Tom Paine's book *The Rights of Man*. Paine was English but had fought alongside Washington. Now he declared that the French Revolution heralded 'an age of revolutions in which everything may be looked for'. He demanded free education, pensions for the old and that every man should have the vote.

However, many people in Britain feared the spread of mob violence and the breakdown of law. Edmund Burke, a Whig MP, argued in his book *Reflections on the Revolution in France* that, instead of freedom, the revolution was creating new tyrants and threatened to bring war to the whole of Europe. Arguments raged to and fro in books, pamphlets and at meetings where they sometimes became violent.

War with France, 1793–1802

Pitt did not want a war with France. War was expensive, disrupted trade and was likely to cause protests against taxes and food shortages. Then, in February 1793, French troops invaded the Netherlands, threatening to block Britain's trade with Europe, much of which was channelled through Dutch ports. Worse, France now controlled the whole coastline facing Britain, the ideal base for an invasion. The Prime Minister had no choice but to to defend Britain and her trade.

This cartoon was published in 1795. To pay for the cost of war against France Pitt was forced to tax, tax and tax again. He trebled taxes on windows, servants, carriages and other luxuries, and introduced a tax on incomes – a shocking novelty that he promised would end after the war.

Pitt knew that Britain could not raise an army large enough to inflict permanent defeat on France in Europe. Instead he did what his father had done in the Seven Years War. He sent Britain's navies to attack French colonies abroad, while Britain's European allies fought the French army. In many cases Britain gave money, known as 'Pitt's Gold', to her allies, to help with the cost of their armies. Unfortunately there was no repeat of 1759, 'the year of victories'.

In 1795 high bread prices and high war taxation caused widespread riots, many with demands for political reforms. A mob stoned the windows of 10 Downing Street, chanting 'No war, no famine, no Pitt, no king'. Pitt decided to crush these critics before they became revolutionaries. Radical societies and meetings of over fifty people were banned, Combination Acts outlawed groups of people combining to form trade unions, and the Act of Habeas Corpus was suspended, allowing anyone suspected of treason to be imprisoned without trial.

By 1796 a new general was winning victory after victory for France's citizen army, the ambitious brilliant Corsican, Napoleon Bonaparte. First he crushed Prussia, then Spain, Holland and Austria. Spain and Holland were forced to re-join the war – this time against Britain. Even Britain's conquests in the West Indies (such as the capture of Trinidad from Spain and Guyana from the Netherlands) were bought at a huge cost. Yellow fever killed 40,000 British soldiers. By 1798 Pitt's government feared that hunger, coupled with the fear of French landings, would lead to risings in support of the revolutionaries.

In fact, the only rebellion was in Ireland, led by the lawyer, Wolfe Tone. He was a Protestant but he was also a revolutionary who wanted to overthrow English rule and end religious discrimination in Ireland. His followers, the United Irishmen, included many Catholics and they waited impatiently for French aid for their cause. When it came in August 1798 it was too late. Government spies had ensured the arrest of Tone, and in June the British had crushed the main force of United Irishmen in the south-east at the Battle of Vinegar Hill.

Pitt reacted to the 1798 rebellion by taking even closer control of Irish affairs. The Act of Union of 1801 abolished Grattan's Dublin Parliament. From now on Ireland was to be represented by Irish MPs at Westminster, where their 100 votes were swamped among a total of 658 MPs. Tone's rebellion had also stirred Protestant fears of Catholic rule. In the 1790s Orange societies (named after the Protestants' hero, William III) were founded, dedicated to maintaining the Protestant supremacy.

Victory at sea

This painting of Napoleon by Jacques David captures Napoleon's energy and personality. There is no sign that he was either short or short sighted, as was popularly believed. Born in 1769 in Corsica, Napoleon joined the French army when he was 16. By the age of 27 he was commanding armies in Italy, and in 1799 he became ruler of France.

Britain's fortune began to turn as her navy won control of the seas. Spanish and Dutch fleets were beaten in battle. In 1798 the French were defeated in Egypt at the Battle of the Nile, leaving Bonaparte and the French army stranded. The hero of the Nile was Horatio Nelson, already famous for his leadership and bravery, having lost his right eye and right arm in battle. At the Battle of Copenhagen in 1801 Nelson defeated the Danish fleet. He had deliberately ignored a signal to withdraw, by putting his telescope to his blind eye saying, 'I have only one eye. I have a right to be blind sometimes. I really do not see the signal.'

By 1802 both enemies needed a breathing space, although they knew the war was not over. They signed the Peace of Amiens. Pitt, too, was exhausted and had resigned as Prime Minister after seventeen years. Despite his harsh treatment of radicals he was respected as 'the pilot who weathered the storm' of French attacks. No one doubted he would be needed again. The French threat would soon return.

Peace lasted for just a year. By 1803 the British once more feared invasion. Across the channel at Boulogne Napoleon's carpenters were building two thousand landing craft for 100,000 French troops. The British prepared their defences, building hilltop beacons to carry warning of invasion to London in just two minutes. Evacuation instructions urged people to take 'all the food in your possession' in readiness for the order to escape from 'Boney's' troops. Weapons were issued to local defence forces.

The invasion threat lasted for two years. Britain's fleets, her 'wooden walls' clung grimly to their task of

Nelson was shot and killed during the Battle of Trafalgar in 1805, aboard HMS Victory. His last battle is famous for his signal to the fleet, 'England expects that every man will do his duty', but it was Nelson's tactics which really won the battle. Instead of the orthodox tactic of sailing parallel to the French fleet, Nelson sailed directly towards them, cutting the French line in two and creating havoc among the enemy. HMS Victory is now docked at Portsmouth.

guarding the Channel and blockading French ships in their ports. The navy saved Britain but the sailors, at sea for two years or more, endured appalling conditions. 'We are looked upon as a dog and not so good. It is worse than a prison', wrote one sailor in 1800. His diet was porridge, salted meat and cheese so hard that it was used to make buttons. Ships' captains kept discipline by flogging sailors with the cat o'nine tails. Sailors died beneath hundreds of lashes, but lack of fresh water and sanitation meant that disease, rather than cannonballs, killed eighty per cent of the casualties in the navy. Over half the crews were conscripts. Each town had to supply its quota of men and they frequently sent, according to Admiral Collingwood, 'the refuse of the gallows and the purgings of the gaol'.

In 1805 the weary contest for control of the seas came to an end. A fleet led by the French Admiral Villeneuve slipped out of harbour and sailed for the West Indies, a decoy to lure the English fleets out of the Channel. The plan failed. The British kept up their blockade and only Nelson's flotilla was sent to hunt Villeneuve. After criss-crossing the Atlantic, Nelson caught the French at Cape Trafalgar off the Spanish coast. On 21 October 1805 Nelson's force destroyed Villeneuve's fleet, killing 4500 French sailors and taking 20,000 prisoners.

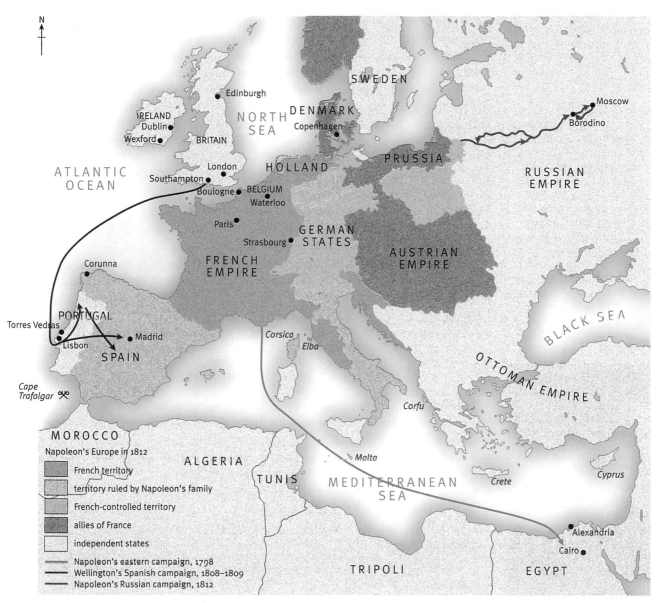

N

Edinburgh

IRELAND
Dublin
Wexford
BRITAIN

SWEDEN

DENMARK
Copenhagen

Moscow
Borodino

NORTH
SEA

PRUSSIA

RUSSIAN
EMPIRE

ATLANTIC
OCEAN

London
Southampton
Boulogne
Paris

HOLLAND

BELGIUM
Waterloo

GERMAN
STATES
Strasbourg

Corunna

PORTUGAL
Torres Vedras
Lisbon
SPAIN

FRENCH
EMPIRE

AUSTRIAN
EMPIRE

BLACK SEA

Madrid

Corsica
Elba

OTTOMAN EMPIRE

Cape
Trafalgar

Corfu

MOROCCO

Napoleon's Europe in 1812

ALGERIA

Malta

Cyprus

French territory

territory ruled by Napoleon's family

TUNIS

MEDITERRANEAN
SEA

Crete

French-controlled territory

allies of France

independent states

Napoleon's eastern campaign, 1798
Wellington's Spanish campaign, 1808–1809
Napoleon's Russian campaign, 1812

TRIPOLI

EGYPT

Alexandria
Cairo

After Trafalgar Napoleon tried to defeat Britain by banning trade between Britain and the countries he had conquered in Europe, shown on this map. However, Britain's navy was too strong for this 'Continental System' to succeed. It continued to move goods into Europe and even opened up new trades, including exports to the people of Spanish America who had thrown off European rule.

A French report in 1811 admitted that stopping British traders was, 'as impossible as to forbid the birds to build their nests'.

On land, however, by 1810 Napoleon's empire stretched over most of Europe. But the Continental System was crumbling, as the Peninsular War drained Napoleon's resources, and he saw that the only way to rebuild it was to crush Russia.

The army and the Peninsular War, 1803–1814

The Battle of Trafalgar ended the threat of invasion, but not the war. Napoleon and his armies still ruled Europe, defeating Britain's allies Austria, Prussia and Russia in massive pitched battles. The best chance for counter-attack lay in the Spanish Peninsula, where Spanish and Portuguese guerrilla forces were attacking the French. In 1808 a British army led by Sir Arthur Wellesley, Viscount Wellington, arrived to reinforce the guerrillas. Wellington's tactics were to drain French military and financial strength. At first he fought a defensive campaign behind the lines of Torres Vedras outside Lisbon, a defensive network of forts, earthworks, moats and rivers. French forces attacked time and time again, but each time they were beaten back.

Slowly, Wellington's tactics showed their effect. When, in 1812, he finally committed his forces to open battle, the Continental System was falling apart. Napoleon saw that to control Europe he had to conquer Russia. In June 1812 he launched 500,000 men against the Tsar. The Russian forces retreated, destroying shelter and food as they went, and even burning Moscow. Napoleon finally caught up with the Russian army at the Battle of Borodino in September, but his soldiers were too exhausted to follow up their victory. As the Russian winter closed in, it was Napoleon's turn to retreat. His men starved or froze to death. Fewer than 50,000 French soldiers returned home.

Napoleon's power had been broken. The Continental System was in ruins. Wellington's army advanced into France. A new alliance of Austria, Prussia, Russia and Sweden defeated Napoleon at the Battle of Leipzig. As the allies occupied Paris in April 1814, Napoleon abdicated. He was exiled to the island of Elba in the Mediterranean.

Waterloo

Within a year Napoleon had escaped. Soldiers flocked to join him. The allies wearily rallied their armies to fight 'the disturber of world repose'. Determined 'to conquer or perish', Napoleon attacked first. His plan was to split the two main bodies of allied troops, the British and the Prussians. On 18 June 1815 Wellington's 67,000 men faced Napoleon's army of 72,000 near the village of Waterloo in Belgium.

The battle lasted from midday to late evening, 'the most desperate business I ever was in' said Wellington. One British soldier described the battlefield,

> ... it was impossible to move a yard without treading upon a wounded comrade, or upon the bodies of the dead, and the loud groans of the wounded and dying was most appalling. At four o'clock our square was a perfect hospital, being full of dead, dying and mutilated soldiers ... the very earth shook under the enormous mass of men and horses.

A French victory seemed likely, until General Blücher's Prussian army arrived. The vital moment came when Napoleon's Imperial Guard attacked but were forced to retreat. '*La Garde recule!*' gasped the rest of the French army in disbelief. From that moment the battle was won but it had been, in Wellington's words, 'the nearest run thing you ever saw in your life'. Survivors gathered, deaf, and bruised by the recoil of their muskets. The wounded were carried on doors or blankets to doctors. There they were gagged, blindfolded and held down while injured limbs were hacked off to prevent death by infection. Legs and arms were piled in heaps.

Throughout the Battle of Waterloo Wellington was in the range of the French guns. At least one bullet missed him only by inches, hitting the right arm of the officer standing on his left. Wellington continued to ride among his men. One wrote, 'the sight of his long nose among us was worth 10,000 men any day of the week'.

Wellington wept when given news of the casualties. 'I don't know what it is to lose a battle', he said, 'but certainly nothing can be more painful than to gain one with the loss of so many of one's friends'. Fifteen thousand of his soldiers were killed; 47,000 died in all. Three days later a young officer, still in his blood-stained uniform, carried the news into London. 'Boney' was beaten. This time Napoleon was exiled to St Helena in the Atlantic where, in 1821, he died.

In 1793 Pitt had gone to war to defend Britain and her trade. He had died in 1806, but he would have approved of the treaties negotiated in 1815 by Viscount Castlereagh, Britain's Foreign Secretary. Castlereagh built up strong buffer states on France's borders, to prevent her from further military adventures. He also insisted that France was not severely punished. He did not want an angry France declaring war once more, in revenge. Further afield, Britain's trade had been successfully defended and the empire had grown, giving new opportunities for colonization and trade. Britain gained Malta – a major base in the Mediterranean – the islands of Trinidad and Tobago in the West Indies, the Cape of Good Hope and Ceylon – two vital staging posts in the trade routes to the east.

The allies' victory over Napoleon confirmed Britain as the world's greatest trading, military and industrial nation. Wellington's troops began the long march home, to a country some had not seen for years and which was changing more rapidly than ever before. To what kind of country were they returning?

Some, but not all, regiments took good care of their men, giving pensions to disabled soldiers. Some awarded medals, agreeing with Sir John Moore that, 'I like to reward bold fellows; it animates the rest'. However, no medals were awarded by the government for the Waterloo campaign until as late as 1847, when half the soldiers who had fought were dead. This is the Waterloo Gold Cross.

(right) 'Load, prime, aim, fire'. To the sound of bellowed orders, soldiers would fire three shots a minute. The noise and confusion was terrifying. So thick was the smoke from muskets that soldiers heard charging horses before they saw them, suddenly appearing only two strides away. As the day wore on, they became deafened by the cannon and muskets, clashing swords, pounding hooves and a sound like 'a violent hailstorm on panes of glass' – bullets hammering on the breastplates of the cavalry.

One-fifth of the soldiers in the British army were Scots. Several Scottish regiments had been founded after the 1745 rebellion, to recruit soldiers from the over-populated Highlands.

CHAPTER 4

Industrial change and political revolution

❖ ─────

In 1804 Benjamin Malkin, a visitor to the South Wales ironworks, described the valleys of South Wales and the house of Richard Crawshay, one of the ironmasters who had transformed the area. His house at Cyfarthfa, wrote Malkin,

> is surrounded with fire, flame, smoke and ashes. The noise of the hammers, rolling mills, forges and bellows incessantly din and crash upon the ear ... The machinery of this establishment is gigantic; and that part of it, worked by water, among the most scientifically curious and mechanically powerful to whom modern improvement has given birth.

Sixty years before, in the 1740s, the valleys Malkin described had been virtually deserted. Merthyr had been a village of farmers and shepherds, typical of Wales, a rural country where villagers added to their income by quarrying, mining and cloth-making. There was no prospect of wealth because manufacturers would not start businesses in a country with only 400,000 people to purchase their wares, half of whom lived on very low wages.

Then, in the late 1750s, the iron-masters arrived, drawn by the coalfields and the fast-flowing streams that would drive their waterwheels. By 1815 Richard Crawshay's Cyfarthfa ironworks at Merthyr Tydfil had become the largest in the world. Crawshay and his neighbours produced over a third of Britain's iron, and in doing so they changed the landscape of South Wales. As recently as the 1770s iron-masters had relied on large numbers of pack horses to take their iron to the coast. Then, led by Crawshay, they built a canal 40 kilometres long to Cardiff, where they built docks and warehouses. Even that could not cope with the quantity of iron produced at Merthyr. By 1802 they had completed a tramroad to Cardiff, along which a horse could haul trucks containing ten tonnes of iron.

Iron was not the only mineral transforming Wales. In the north the mines of Anglesey were producing thirty per cent of Britain's copper. Improved roads and canals carried Welsh tin-plate and slate from sea-ports to destinations all over Britain. Welsh-made cloth was being used for the uniforms of the soldiers fighting Napoleon.

The story was repeated throughout Britain. For the first time in the history of the world a country was being revolutionized by its industries. Iron, coal and textiles were changing the pattern of the country's wealth and population. Lancashire and Yorkshire replaced East Anglia and the south-west of England as the major cloth-making regions. The iron industry moved north from Sussex and the Forest of Dean to the coalfields of the midlands, Scotland and Wales. The regions which had traditionally been the poor, underpopulated fringes of British life were transformed; they became the crowded centres of wealth and vitality.

Britain's industries poured out cannon, muskets and ammunition to help her to win the war against France. Other nations bought her textiles, pottery, iron-ware and even steam engines. However, this increase in trade and wealth had its price. Old ways disappeared as the new industries demanded new patterns of working, often making life harsher. No one suffered more than the children of the poor.

A watercolour painting by George Robertson of Richard Crawshay's Nant-y-glo ironworks in 1788.

By 1800 the once-rural village of Merthyr was a growing town at the centre of the South Wales coalfield and iron industry. Over 7500 people (Cardiff had only 2000) lived in rickety buildings and cramped stone cottages, lit up each night by the 'furnaces and truly volcanic accumulation of blazing cinders'.

STEAM

Since the early 1700s steam engines had been used to pump water out of mines, but the power to turn the wheels which drove the machinery in iron foundries and textile workshops was provided by humans, animals or water.

In 1765 James Watt, a scientific instrument maker in Glasgow, was asked to repair a model of a steam engine. He discovered ways to make it work much more powerfully, but with much less fuel. Now he needed to find a partner with some money to spend on building a full-sized engine. In 1775 he joined forces with a Birmingham manufacturer, Matthew Boulton. At Boulton's Soho works in Birmingham, his engineers provided the skills needed to build the

▲ *A Boulton and Watt steam engine of 1788. Important though it was, the steam engine did not dominate industry immediately. Boulton and Watt patented their design, stopping other manufacturers making similar engines until 1800. They only made twelve engines a year, and only the larger firms could afford or needed them. After 1800, other people began making steam engines.*

▲ *A pit-head scene painted in about 1820. The steam engine hauled coal and miners up the mine shaft, but horses still played an important part, carrying coal from the pit-head.*

Steam-powered threshing machines, to separate out the grain from the straw, were very useful to farmers, but threatened to put farm labourers out of work. In 1830 The Gentleman's Magazine described 'the outrageous conduct of agricultural mobs of the lower classes going about demolishing the threshing machines'.

machine Watt had designed. By 1781 Boulton and Watt had made an engine that could turn wheels.

In 1838 a book on industry in Britain described the transformation the steam engine had caused:

Steam Engines … create a vast demand for fuel; and, while they lend their powerful arms to drain the pits and to raise the coals, they call into employment multitudes of miners, engineers, shipbuilders and sailors, and cause the construction of canals and railways.

The first steam locomotive, designed by Richard Trevithick, ran on the Merthyr Tydfil train road in 1804. In 1809 Trevithick brought an improved locomotive to London, where he built a circular track on which to run it. He called the engine 'Catch-Me-Who-Can', charged people a shilling to see it and offered rides at twelve miles per hour, for those brave enough to accept. Trevithick's idea, to make a steam engine run on rails pulling a load, was developed by others after he died.

In 1839 the artist J.M.W. Turner painted this picture, The Fighting Temeraire. *The hulk of an old sailing ship, the Temeraire, is being towed by a steam-driven tug. Turner is looking back to the age of sail, and captures the new power of steam.*

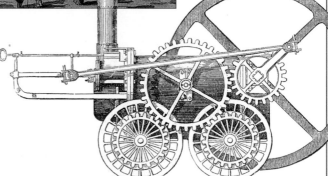

Factories played a vital part in the textile industries but, even in 1850, only six out of every hundred workers were employed in factories, and most employed fewer than a hundred people. There were many workshops like this loom shop at Rawtenstall in Lancashire, probably built in about 1780. Such workshops were a halfway stage between 'domestic' workshops, which had been part of people's houses, and factories.

From workhouse child to factory worker

In 1799 seven-year-old Robert Blincoe was 'inspired ... with new life and spirits'. In the St Pancras workhouse in London there were rumours that Robert and other homeless children were to be apprenticed at a textile mill in Nottingham. There they would 'be transformed into ladies and gentlemen; ... be fed on roast beef and plum pudding ... have silver watches and plenty of cash in their pockets'. Part of the rumour was true. In August eighty children set off in new clothes, each with 'a shilling ... a new pocket handkerchief and a large piece of gingerbread'. They travelled in two large wagons, with clean straw for beds. The doors were locked.

When Robert arrived at the mill the first words he heard were, 'God help the poor wretches', 'The Lord have mercy on them'. That night Robert 'could not restrain his tears'. For the next fourteen years he worked twelve hours a day, with one hour's break. If his work was poor he was punished by having 'two hand-vices of a pound weight each ... screwed to my ears'. On other occasions 'three or four of us have been hung at once on a cross-beam above the machinery, hanging by our hands, without shirts or stockings'.

Accidents were common. Workers lost limbs in the machinery when they stumbled with tiredness. 'One girl, Mary Richards, was made a cripple ... lapped up by a strap underneath the drawing frame'. Robert survived to tell his story in 1833 to a Parliamentary Commission on *The Employment of Children in Manufactories*. He was one of the lucky ones.

An engraving showing female factory workers, published in 1835 in a book about the history of cotton manufacture by Edward Baines, who approved of the new factories.

Arkwright, Strutt and other factory owners employed children and women. They were smaller and nimbler than men around the machinery, could be paid less (women were paid only two-thirds of men's wages) and were thought less likely to complain about poor conditions.

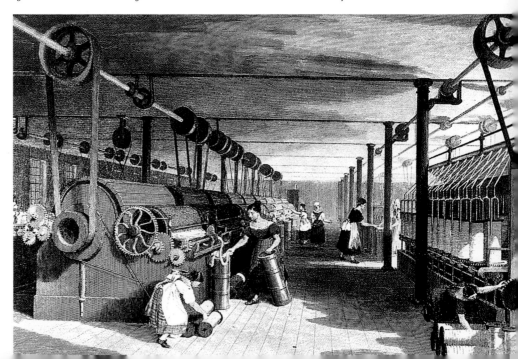

Not a spark of pity was shown to the sick of either sex; they worked to the very last moment ... and when it was no longer possible, if they dropped down, they were put into a wheelbarrow and wheeled to the Prentice house ... where they were left to live or die.

Conditions were just as awful in other new industries. Many people were shocked by a report on the coal industry in Scotland in 1812. It described how,

An illustration for Frances Trollope's The Life and Adventures of Michael Armstrong, the Factory Boy *published in the 1840s. The story is about the appalling conditions endured by a factory boy, which the author said she wrote, 'to drag into the light of day the hideous mass of injustice and suffering to which thousands of infant labourers are subjected'.*

the mother ... descends the pit with her elder daughters, when each, having a basket of a suitable form lays it down, and into it the large coals were rolled; ... it frequently takes two men to lift the burden upon their backs ... the mother sets out first carrying a lighted candle in her teeth; the girls follow ... with weary steps and slow ascend the stairs ... it is no uncommon thing to see them when ascending the pit, weeping most bitterly, from the excessive severity of their labour ...

Not every factory owner and employer was so harsh. Many followed the example of the first great factory owner, Richard Arkwright, of Cromford Mill near Derby (see page 16) and his partner, Jedediah Strutt. Neither would allow cruelty. Even so, Arkwright at first employed children aged seven, but after 1806 he would only employ those over ten so that, he said, 'they might learn to read before they came'.

Some of the first factory employers believed they should be responsible for their employees' general well-being. Wedgwood built well-lit two-storey houses near his factory. Each house had two bedrooms, a kitchen and an outside lavatory. For every dozen houses there was a water pump. Arkwright was unusual in providing entertainment as well as housing. In September each year, at the festival of 'candlelighting', workers were given buns, nuts, fruit and ale after parading around the village. He also gave bonuses to the best workers.

Arkwright and Strutt, as well as others, were proud of their factories and the care they took of their workers. There was nothing new about children or women working. Strutt pointed out that, 'many, indeed most of the females, have been previously employed, some even from five years old, at lace running or tambouring'.

Arkwright's workers were the first to experience factory life, and he and other new mill-owners relied on a system of punishments to control them. Anyone not at work when the factory bell sounded was fined. At Strutt's mill the 'forfeit' list of fines paid by mill hands included 'riding on each other's back' and 'terrifying S. Pearson with her ugly face'.

During the Napoleonic wars many landowners were able to charge high prices for their crops and animals. Some, like the Duke of Bedford and Thomas Coke, held sheep-shearing festivals, inviting other landowners to share their new ideas about farming and to buy breeding animals from them. Other farmers were slow to change their tools or machinery, partly because there were plenty of labourers who could be paid low wages. In 1801 about a third of the working population was still employed in farming.

In the early 1700s Defoe had written that there was nothing 'more frequent than for an Englishman to work until he had got his pockets full of money, and then to go and be idle or perhaps drunk till 'tis all gone'. Workers who celebrated a day off work on Sunday frequently worshipped 'St Monday' in order to recover. Factories forced workers to change their habits as well as their workplaces and homes. If they were not at work on Monday they risked losing their jobs. During the day their work was overseen, their breaks timed. One song of the time lamented,

> Oh happy man, Oh happy thou,
> While toiling at thy spade and plough
> While thou amidst thy pleasures roll,
> All at thy labour uncontrolled:
> Here at the mills in pressing crowds
> The high-built chimneys puff black clouds
> And all around the slaves do dwell
> Who're called to labour by a bell.

Filth and disease

Despite the harsh working conditions, families flocked to work in the developing industries. Wages were higher and employment more regular than in the countryside. However, their new homes in the growing centres of the new industries were often as grim as the worst factories. The long hours demanded by the owners left them little time to walk long distances each morning, so they lived crammed together, close to the factories or workshops. Many young newcomers were forced to settle for a cheap lodging house. In Leeds such houses averaged nine beds to a room and, it was reported, five lodgers to a bed. Water came from taps at street corners and sewage was piled high against house walls. In Merthyr the cottages of iron-workers and miners, according to Benjamin Malkin,

were most of them built in scattered confusion without any order or plan. As the works increased more cottages were wanted, and erected in spaces between those that had been previously built ... these streets are now many in number, close and confined, ... very filthy for the most part and doubtless very unhealthy.

The new industrial towns were breeding grounds for diseases. Epidemics of typhus, measles, dysentery, influenza and other diseases killed thousands, and little could be done to stop them. No one knew how infections spread. In 1774 an Edinburgh doctor reported an outbreak of puerperal fever in the infirmary, 'almost every woman, as soon as she was delivered [of her baby] ... was seized with it; and all of them died, though every method was tried to cure the disorder'.

Disease was not the only terror. There were no anaesthetics, apart from alcohol or drugs such as opium, so that pain was uncontrollable. Only the most desperate operations were carried out. Josiah Wedgwood survived the amputation of his leg. Many patients did not. Shock or infection killed them.

Towns in Britain in 1790

● towns with 16,000–50,000 people
● towns with over 50,000 people

0   100   200 km

(above) By 1790 Britain's largest towns were no longer in the rich agricultural country of midland and southern England. They had been overtaken by the growing trading and manufacturing centres of the north, south Wales and Scotland, and by the ports on the Atlantic coast.

(right) Most people blamed disease on 'bad air'. This is understandable given the smoke and fog in the cities.

As coal burning increased, engineers saw the possibility of using waste gases to produce light. The first system for piping gas to jets was made by William Murdoch, foreman at the iron foundry of Boulton & Watts in Cornwall. In the early 1800s a few factories adopted gas lighting, and in 1812 a private company took the first gas lighting to some London streets.

In 1810 the novelist Fanny Burney was discovered to have breast cancer. The only means to save her life was a mastectomy, removal of the breast. Nine months later she described the operation in a letter,

> the Bed stead was instantly surrounded by the seven men and my nurse. I refused to be held; but when, Bright through the cambric, I saw the glitter of polished steel – I closed my eyes ... when the dreadful steel was plunged into the breast – cutting through veins – arteries – flesh – nerves – I needed no injunctions not to restrain my cries. I began a scream that lasted unintermittingly during the whole time.

However in 1796 one important breakthrough in medicine was made when a Gloucestershire doctor, Edward Jenner, examined eight-year-old James Phipps. He took out his knife, and scratched James's arm. Then he infected the scratch with pus from a victim of one of the most virulent diseases in the world, smallpox. Days went by, then weeks, but James did not develop the tell-tale smallpox sores. Jenner was overjoyed. He already knew that dairymaids did not catch smallpox, and reasoned that this was because they had first had cowpox, a much less serious disease and therefore developed an immunity to the more deadly disease. Several weeks before he infected James with smallpox, he had given him cowpox. Now James too was immune to the deadly disease. Jenner had proved that smallpox could be prevented. Vaccination (so-called because the

Vaccination was not popular with everyone. In 1802 the Anti-Vaccine Society published this cartoon by James Gillray, ridiculing Jenner's ideas. People who were fearful of vaccination still used traditional remedies for smallpox, such as applying boiled turnips to the feet.

Latin word for cow is *vacca)* spread worldwide. In 1802 Thomas Jefferson, President of the United States, wrote to Jenner that medicine had 'never before produced any single improvement of such utility ... Mankind can never forget that you have lived'. But, important though Jenner's discovery was, he did not understand precisely why his method worked. No one yet knew that diseases were caused by bacteria and so they continued to rage, unstoppable amid the filth of the growing towns.

'Apply to General Ludd'

By 1811 Napoleon's Continental System (see page 39) had forced manufacturers to either lay off workers or reduce wages. With poor harvests came fear and starvation. In Carlisle three hundred men and women broke into warehouses and carried off all the food they could find. Magistrates called in the army. As women and boys threw stones at the soldiers, shots were fired. One woman was killed and several were wounded. Such incidents, caused by hunger, had become common.

> Chant no more your old rhymes about bold Robin Hood,
> His feats I but little admire.
> I will sing the Achievements of General Ludd,
> Now the hero of Nottinghamshire.

Attacks by knitters began in the Nottingham stocking industry in 1811. Their targets were the stocking-frames on which cheap goods were made in return for low wages. Small bands of skilled workers attacked at night, leaving behind threatening messages signed by General Ludd, King Ludd or Ned Ludd, so they became known as Luddites, although there was probably no such man. The attacks spread to the textile districts of Yorkshire and Lancashire. By the end of 1811 the *Leeds Mercury* declared, 'the Insurrectional state to which this county has been reduced ... has no parallel in history, since the troubled days of Charles the First'.

In April 1812 Luddites launched one of their most desperate raids, on Cartwright's mill at Rawfolds, near Huddersfield. One hundred and fifty armed men attacked the mill, which was heavily guarded. Under heavy fire the Luddites tried to break down the mill doors, but they were forced to retreat, leaving hammers, axes, muskets, pikes and two of their comrades. Both men died. Seventeen others were later executed.

The government saw the beginnings of revolution in these attacks. In the six years following Pitt's death one Prime Minister had quickly followed another. Spencer Perceval became the third and, when he was assassinated in the House of Commons in May 1812 by a bankrupt merchant, crowds paraded around Nottingham 'with drums beating and flags flying in triumph'. In the Potteries the news was carried by a man 'leaping into the air, waving his hat round his head, and shouting with

An anti-slavery medallion produced by Wedgwood in about 1790. The campaign, involving evangelicals such as Wilberforce, succeeded in 1807 in abolishing slave-trading by British merchants and in British ships. However, the trade continued for many years in ships of other nations and slavery itself continued in Britain's colonies until 1834.

Many children learned to read and write at dame schools such as this one, shown in a painting made in about 1845. They were set up by women in their own homes who charged weekly fees but often did not teach the children very much.

Perhaps children learned more at Sunday schools. Evangelical Christians were great supporters of education. Between 1780 and 1820 8000 Sunday schools were opened, where children were taught to read the Bible and other improving books. Their other purpose was to 'civilize' the poor without giving them the skills to try to change the world. Hannah More and others agreed that writing was an unnecessary and dangerous skill for the poor to have.

frantic joy, "Perceval is shot, Hurrah!"'. In Leeds a leaflet was published which encouraged people to rebel against the king and the government,

> You are requested to come forward with Arms and help the Redressers to redress their Wrongs and shake off the hateful Yoke of a Silly Old Man, and his Son more silly and their Rogueish Ministers, all Nobles and Tyrants, must be brought down ... Above 40,000 Heroes are ready to break out, to crush the old Government and establish a new one. Apply to General Ludd.

Repression

After Perceval's death in May 1812, his successor as Prime Minister was Robert Jenkinson, Lord Liverpool. He remained Prime Minister until 1827. Immediately he took over, Liverpool faced the same choice as Pitt had in 1795. Should he give more help to the poor, and more people the right to vote, or should he stop and repress all opposition and criticism? In the midst of war, Liverpool, like Pitt, chose repression.

Those who believed that no help should be given to the unemployed and the very poor received support from the ideas of Thomas Malthus. In 1798 Malthus had published an *Essay on the Principle of Population*. He was inspired by the fear that population growth would outstrip the supply of food. He believed that 'man's perpetual tendency ... to increase beyond the means of subsistence' meant that checks to population growth such as war and famine were essential to avoid disaster. Malthus said there should be no poor relief, no workhouses. They only encouraged the poor to have families. If necessary the poor must be allowed to starve.

Even more influential were the ideas of the economist, Adam Smith, who argued that trade and industry flourished when manufacturers could produce goods efficiently and cheaply, without interference. He criticized tariffs, the taxes that each country put on imported goods, because this raised prices of imported goods and allowed British manufacturers to keep their prices high. Employers and landowners used Smith's ideas to argue that combinations (the name given to early trades unions) and minimum wage-rates should be outlawed to help them cut costs. Lord Liverpool's government agreed. They did away with many old laws dating from Elizabethan times which had protected minimum wage-rates, and they banned combinations. Twelve thousand soldiers were sent north in 1812 to put an end to Luddism, more men than Wellington commanded in Spain. Anyone who criticized the government could be arrested as a traitor.

Radical societies were forced to use cellars and the dark corners of taverns for meeting places. Some hatched wild schemes to assassinate George III, but most planned for a better future. In 1795 many had heard the radical speaker and writer, John Thelwall, speak of a time when a worker in the Spitalfields silk industry had,

The number of newspapers in Britain was increasing rapidly. By the 1830s there were over 130 local newspapers. Many shared radical ideas. The Exchange Herald *was founded in Manchester in 1809, the* Manchester Guardian *in 1821 to 'warmly advocate the cause of reform'. The* Scotsman *was founded in 1817.*

generally, beside the apartment in which he carried out his vocation, a small summer house and a narrow slip of garden, at the outskirts of the town, where he spent his Monday, either in flying his pigeons or raising his tulips. But those gardens are now fallen into decay ... and you will find the poor weavers and their families crowded together in vile, filthy and unwholesome chambers, destitute of the most common comforts, and even of the common necessaries of life.

In 1815 workers in both the new factories and the older trades, such as the hand-loom weavers, carpenters, shoe-makers, tailors, framework knitters and lacemakers, still dreamed of a return to those better days. As twenty years of war ended there were celebrations in the streets. People looked forward to a future in which wages would rise, bread would be cheaper and they could speak of reforms without fear of government spies accusing them of treason. Within weeks stones were once again being hurled at the windows of the Prime Minister's house at 10 Downing Street, in London.

CHAPTER 5

After Waterloo – fighting for power

❖

It was a hot, sunny day on 16 August 1819. Along the dusty roads into Manchester, from Bolton, Oldham and other mill towns, came cheerful processions of men, women and children, marching to the sound of brass bands. They carried banners proclaiming 'Liberty', 'Votes for All' and 'No Corn Laws'. Already that summer, radical leaders had held meetings in Leeds, Birmingham and London. They were only the latest of many demonstrations which had taken place since 1815.

Throughout those years bread prices had been high. Most people blamed the Corn Laws, introduced by Parliament to stop imports of cheap foreign corn. Without foreign competition landowners had sold their crops at high prices which meant that bread prices had stayed high. Many were without work. With the war at an end, those making weapons and uniforms lost their jobs or had their wages cut. Returning soldiers could not find work. Anger and starvation led to riots which Lord Liverpool and his ministers suppressed, sending in soldiers to break up protests. However repression only increased support for radical ideas. Many people, like those gathering at St Peter's Field, Manchester, believed that their lives would only improve when ordinary people could vote.

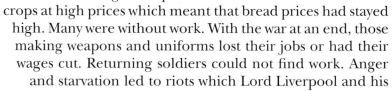

William Cobbett, journalist and radical. According to Samuel Bamford, a Lancashire radical, Cobbett's writings, 'were read on nearly every cottage hearth … he directed his readers to the true cause of their sufferings – misgovernment; and to its proper corrective – parliamentary reform.' Cobbett's newspaper, the Political Register, *and other radical papers such as the* Black Dwarf *were read aloud in taverns.*

Peterloo

As many as 60,000 people were packed into St Peter's Field when Henry 'Orator' Hunt began his speech, demanding the vote for all men. Hunt had been speaking for ten minutes when the crowd heard shouts of 'the Soldiers!'. The magistrates had ordered the troops to arrest Hunt. As the soldiers pressed through the throng, people panicked and ran. A Lancashire man, Samuel Bamford, who was one of the leaders, described what happened next,

> Sabres were plied to hew a way through naked held-up hands and defence-less heads; and then chopped limbs and wound-gaping skulls were seen and groans and cries were mingled with the din of that horrid confusion.

This cartoon, Manchester Heroes, by the satirist and illustrator George Cruikshank, published in 1819, was one of many that sympathized with the victims of Peterloo. Liverpool and his ministers were certainly hated. The Foreign Secretary, Lord Castlereagh, described by a colleague as 'a splendid summit of bright and polished frost', was reviled by the poet Byron as a 'cold-blooded … miscreant'. To another poet, Shelley, 'murder … had a mask like Castlereagh'.

Altogether, eleven people were killed and about four hundred wounded. This horror was quickly dubbed the Peterloo Massacre, in ironic reference to Wellington's triumph in 1815.

However no armed rising followed Peterloo. Extremists wanted revolution but there were too many groups with different aims. More importantly, as a Manchester newspaper, the *Exchange Herald*, reported, 'trade seems progressively improving and the poor weavers … begin to feel the good effects by an increase … in their too scanty wages'. Better-fed workers no longer attended protest meetings. As harvests improved, bread prices fell. William Cobbett had said that 'you cannot agitate a man on a full stomach'. Liverpool, his ministers and the country's landowners breathed sighs of relief.

Robert Peel was one of the most able politicians of the century, but also a shy, awkward man who did not win friends easily. Lord Shaftesbury described him as 'an iceberg with a slight thaw on the surface', and even when he was Prime Minister in the 1840s an observer described how, when Peel entered the House of Commons, 'he looks at no one, recognizes no one, receives salutation from no one. He seems neither to know or to be known by any member present'.

Peelers, prisons and a royal scandal

Although the riots died down Lord Liverpool and his young Home Secretary, Robert Peel, still believed they faced an increase in crime. Many criminals felt safe because jurors refused to convict thieves for small thefts because the punishment was death. Peel therefore cut the number of crimes punishable by death, hoping that more criminals would be convicted. When this happened, the increase in convicted criminals made another problem worse. Already over 3000 were transported to Australia each year, while others spent their sentences in a prison ship, or 'hulk', moored in a river estuary. But each year that still left tens of thousands in the jails which were often run as private ventures.

Peel began to reform the prison system, spurred on by Evangelical Christians such as the Quaker, Elizabeth Fry. Prisoners were separated from each other and women warders looked after female prisoners. However they were still condemned to harsh physical labour, stepping on treadmills or turning crank handles.

In 1829 Peel also created the first real police force for London. The 'Peelers' or 'Bobbies' did reduce crime, but many people opposed them, believing that the police were a threat to their liberties.

The hard-drinking and extravagant King George IV (1820-1830) presented another problem for Lord Liverpool. Deeply unpopular, the king was, in the words of one newspaper, 'over head and heels in debt and disgrace ... a man who has just closed half a century without one single claim on the gratitude of his country'. In 1820 he created a huge public scandal when he tried to divorce his wife, Caroline. The crowds cheered Caroline and jeered George, and when George asked Parliament to grant him a divorce the vote went against him. Part of the king's problem was that he could no longer buy support from politicians with well-paid but work-free official jobs. During the war with France, Pitt had scrapped many of these posts to save money. Equally important, George lacked the energy to battle with his Prime Minister. In 1822 Liverpool appointed George Canning as Foreign Secretary, even though the king detested him because he had supported Caroline. When Liverpool finally retired in 1827 George even suggested that the Cabinet should choose the new Prime Minister. This did not spell the end of royal power, but much had changed since 1783 when George III had astonished and defeated the politicians by making Pitt Prime Minister.

An illustration of Elizabeth Fry, published in 1820. In 1813 she visited Newgate prison in London. There she saw 300 women, many with children, who, she wrote, 'all slept on the floor; at times one hundred and twenty in one ward … Everything was filthy to excess, and the smell was disgusting'.

She set to work to improve conditions. She started a school for the children and took in second-hand clothing for the prisoners. Women were put to work making clothes for convicts in Australia, while she or her friends read the Bible to them. Swearing, gambling and quarrelling were forbidden.

A more united kingdom?

In the early nineteenth century the coalfields, ironworks and textile mills of Scotland and South Wales played as large a part in the Industrial Revolution as those in the English midlands and north. Better trade and communications were drawing the different parts of Britain closer together, but there were still important national differences.

Although the Welsh gentry followed fashion and spoke English, over three quarters of Welsh people spoke Welsh as their only language, described in 1759 by the poet Richard Rolt as,

A language fit for angels; graceful, rich,
Gay, copious and sublime; transcending far
The voice of nature spoken in other climes.

Many people fought hard to keep the Welsh culture alive. Local printing presses produced Bibles and poetry and printed Welsh music. *Eisteddfodau* (meetings of poets and musicians at which they celebrated their language and culture) were revived in the 1700s. Many children were taught to read and write in their own language in the circulating schools, begun by Griffiths Jones in 1731. Travelling teachers would stay in a village for three or four months at a time, teaching local children in the church, a barn or farmhouse, timing their visits to fit in with the quieter parts of the agricultural year so that children could attend.

In Scotland the Gaelic language had been under attack since the 1600s because the English connected it with disorder and later with Catholicism. The Scottish Society for the Propagation of Christian Knowledge started nearly two hundred schools to teach English. Again circulating schools fought back, teaching children in Gaelic, but even the Edinburgh Gaelic Schools' Society admitted in 1829 that, 'so ignorant be the parents that it is difficult to convince them that it can be of any benefit to their children to learn Gaelic, though they are all anxious … to have them taught English.'

Some forces were too strong for the supporters of Welsh and Gaelic. In the 1790s landowners in the Highlands, eager to use their land for grazing sheep, began to clear out the crofters who had grown crops in fenced fields near their cottages. After 1815 these 'clearances' became widespread. In the words of an eyewitness, the landowners used, 'every imaginable means, short of sword or musket … to drive the Highlanders away, to force them to exchange their farms and comfortable cottages, built by themselves or their forefathers, for inhospitable rocks on the seashore … Many deaths followed from alarm, fatigue, cold.' Thousands of crofters had their homes burned. Some perished, others made for Glasgow and other industrial towns, or for America.

In Ireland industrial change came slowly. Farming remained the way of life for most of its eight million inhabitants. The poorest tenant farmers were dependent on the single, but nourishing, potato crop. Industrial development was concentrated around Belfast, where the need for ships during the French wars led to growth in the shipbuilding industry. The linen trade

A painting of Trinity College, Dublin in 1790, by James Malton. In the mid-eighteenth century Dublin's population had been second only to London, thanks to trade and the presence of the Irish Parliament. 'There is gaiety, pleasure, luxury and extravagance', wrote Arthur Young after visiting the city. 'Every night in winter there is a ball or party'. Yet by 1820 Dublin was emptying, its Georgian mansions taken over by poor families from the countryside. Since the Act of Union had been passed in 1800 many society families had drifted away from Dublin, often to London.

Daniel O'Connell, who called Wellington and Peel 'the most bitter persevering and unmitigated enemies of the Catholics'. In 1815 O'Connell and Peel nearly fought a duel when O'Connell accused Peel, the government minister responsible for Ireland, of insulting him. On the day of the duel O'Connell was arrested, but the two men rearranged the duel in the Netherlands. Again O'Connell was arrested, and both men were warned that if one was killed the other would be hanged. They abandoned their plans but the hatred persisted.

flourished, transforming Dunmanway, for example, from a poor village in the 1740s to one filled a decade later with prosperous, well-dressed people with 'neither a family nor loom unemployed' according to the Inspector to the Linen Board, Robert Stephenson.

However, prosperity could not remove the resentment at the fact that ninety per cent of Irish people – the Catholic population – could not vote or stand for Parliament. When the harvests failed, as they did in 1817, 1823 and again in 1826, it seemed to many that the first step to relieving the dreadful poverty in Ireland was to send MPs to Westminster who understood their needs. In the 1820s they found the champion they needed in Daniel O'Connell, a Dublin lawyer with immense energy, daring and a voice 'you could hear a mile off, as if it were coming through honey'.

Victory for 'The Great Dan'

O'Connell took on the leadership of the Catholic Association, into whose campaign fund thousands of peasants and townspeople paid a penny a month, trusting the 'Great Dan' to deliver them from poverty. O'Connell's objective was Catholic Emancipation – freedom from the laws which prevented them from voting or standing for Parliament. He believed that once there were Catholics in the House of Commons the government would be forced to pass laws to improve the lives of the Irish poor.

O'Connell's chance to challenge the government came at an election at County Clare in the west of Ireland. As a Catholic in 1828 it was against the law for him to become an MP, but even so he stood for election against the local Protestant landlord. It was a triumph. He won the most votes, creating a dilemma for Wellington (who had recently become Prime Minister) and Peel. If they let O'Connell become an MP they would betray their own beliefs, promises and the trust of their supporters. If they refused, O'Connell would lead a rent-strike throughout Ireland, and perhaps a national rebellion.

Wellington and Peel decided they had no choice. They persuaded the near-hysterical George IV that the laws against Catholics must go. Immediately radical Tories damned Wellington and Peel as 'rats prepared to throw overboard every principle'. In Ireland O'Connell was proclaimed 'The Liberator', but his work was not yet over. He now set about a campaign to repeal the Act of Union and give back to the Irish their own Parliament.

*Before the 1832 Reform Act
many of the towns and ports
that were creating Britain's
wealth had no MPs to
represent them in Parliament.
The distribution of MPs had
changed little since the Middle
Ages. For example, the county
and boroughs of Cornwall
had 44 MPs, one more than
for the whole of Scotland.
Wales had only 27 MPs, but
Ireland had had 100 since
the Act of Union in 1800.*

Reform or revolution?

The year after O'Connell's triumph, Wellington and Peel faced another crisis in southern England. In 1830 high food prices and unemployment once again sparked riots across the farming districts. Most rioters were simply demanding regular work and food for their families. Other people, mostly in the industrial areas, believed that to relieve the causes of poverty there had to be political reform. Radical groups revived. In 1829 Thomas Attwood, a banker, founded the Birmingham Political Union. Attwood declared that Parliament, 'in its present state is evidently too far removed … from the wants and interests of the lower and middle classes to have … any close identity of feeling with them'.

The answer, said the National Union of Working Classes, a London organization of artisan radicals which published the *Poor Man's Guardian*, was reform, 'annual parliaments, extension of the franchise to every adult male, vote by [secret] ballot and especially no property qualification for members of Parliament'. They believed these reforms would ensure that all men could vote without fear of threats or bribes, that ordinary men could become MPs, and that governments would listen to the voters or they would quickly lose at the next election. Women were not included. At Attwood's first meeting he drew 15,000 people. Soon nearly every town had its own political union and the great provincial newspapers such as the *Leeds Mercury* and the *Manchester Guardian* joined the demand for reform. Working class and middle class united in demanding an end to rule by a small group of aristocratic landowners.

Aberdeen

SCOTLAND

Dundee
Perth

Glasgow

IRELAND

Bradford Leeds
Blackburn
Bolton Halifax
Oldham Sheffield
Macclesfield

Wolverhampton Birmingham

WALES ENGLAND

Cheltenham
Merthyr
Tydfil Stroud
Swansea
Cardiff
Greenwich

Brighton
Portsmouth

Devonport

MPs before 1832

▢ half of all MPs came from this area

• large towns with no MP

● rotten and pocket boroughs

0   100   200 km

Wellington, still the Prime Minister, opposed any reform, but he was isolated among leading politicians. He resigned and the new king, William IV (1830–1837) called on Lord Grey, leader of the Whigs, to become Prime Minister. Immediately Grey introduced bills for electoral reform, but they were thrown out by the House of Lords. The reaction was violent. In Bristol a local parson, the Reverend Jackson, recorded that in October 1831,

> the multitude assembled before the Mansion House in Queen Square, and smashed the windows by a volley of stones … about four o'clock we saw the new City and County gaol in flames … Other property to an immense amount is also destroyed.

Nottingham Castle, the home of the Duke of Newcastle, was burned by crowds who believed, like Cobbett, that the bill would,

> put bread and cheese into [a labouring man's] satchel instead of infernal cold potatoes … a bottle of beer to carry in the field instead of making him lie down on his belly and drink out of the brook.

In May 1832 Grey's third Reform Bill was rejected by the Lords. Grey resigned. The king asked Wellington to return as Prime Minister.

Once again Britain seemed on the brink of rebellion. In Birmingham it was reported that Attwood would lead 200,000 people to London and camp there until the Bill was passed. The soldiers of the Scots Greys Regiment were ordered to 'rough-sharpen' their sabres in preparation for stopping the march, but they sent messages to reformers and to the government telling them that they would refuse to stop a peaceful march. Events moved quickly. Wellington could not find enough supporters to form a government. The king turned reluctantly again to Grey, who was now strong enough to demand a promise from the king to create enough new Whig peers to vote the third Reform Bill through the Lords. The Lords backed down (not wishing to be swamped by large numbers of reforming Whig peers) and passed the Bill, which became the Reform Act of 1832.

However, 'the great bill for giving everybody everything' was nothing of the kind. All along Grey had intended 'to preserve and not to overthrow', by uniting the middle class with the aristocracy. The new Act created 280,000 new electors but only gave the vote to men who owned property worth £10 a year or more, a sum which would exclude the miners, weavers, factory hands and ironworkers. Grey's Act did give many industrial cities their own MPs for the first time, but of Birmingham's 144,000 people only 7000 were rich enough to vote. In Leeds only 5000 could vote, out of a population of 125,000. None of them were women.

The rising sun in Gillray's 1832 cartoon echoed reformers' hopes. In 1832 the Leeds Mercury *rejoiced in 'The Victory of the People'. Cobbett hailed 'the commencement of a mighty revolution'. In Derbyshire the industrialist Jedediah Strutt entertained 1000 women workers with a dance and dinner: '4800 lbs of beef, 3184 lbs of plum pudding, 7000 loaves and 2550 quarts of ale' were provided according to the* Derby Mercury. *Elsewhere stones were thrown at the king at the Ascot races, and after the Act was passed Wellington was taunted by a mob shouting 'Bonaparte for ever', and had to be rescued by a group of policemen.*

Michael Faraday's first job had been as an apprentice bookbinder. A customer noticed his interest in science and gave him a ticket to hear a lecture by Sir Humphrey Davy. Faraday took notes, then sent them to Davy, who was so impressed he gave Faraday a job as an assistant in the Royal Institution. Faraday became Director in 1826, when he also began the Royal Institution Christmas lectures, which are still held every year.

Among the new inventions were miners' lamps which replaced candles and so cut the risk of explosions down the mine. Both Sir Humphrey Davy and George Stephenson developed successful lamps in 1815.

The magical machine

In 1831, amid the reform debates, Michael Faraday remained in his laboratory, convinced that he could use magnets to produce electricity. His experiments worked, and he went on to discover how to make an electrical motor and generator. Faraday was not an industrialist, but a scientist, interested in discoveries for their own sake. Having made this remarkable discovery, instead of working on how to apply it he immediately set to work on a new scientific problem. It would be many years before electricity transformed Britain.

Meanwhile, engineers were making improvements to Boulton and Watt's early steam-driven engines. One improvement, developed by Richard Trevithick in 1804, was the building of a steam locomotive, a steam engine mounted on wheels used to haul wagons along iron rails.

In the north of England mining companies were also looking for ways of pulling heavier loads than horses could manage. Their engineers copied Trevithick's idea and in 1814 George Stephenson, an engineer at a Northumberland colliery, built his first locomotive.

Stephenson was already planning a railway to take a mixture of horse and locomotive-drawn freight from the south Durham coalfields to the port of Stockton. When the Stockton-Darlington railway opened in 1825 it attracted the attention of a group of south Lancashire manufacturers who wanted something faster than barges for transporting their goods and raw materials, which in winter could be frozen in the ice for weeks at a time. They invited Stephenson to supervise the construction of the new Liverpool to Manchester railway line.

Few people thought that steam locomotives were the best form of rail haulage. These early engines often broke down, and they used huge, expensive quantities of coal. As the Liverpool to Manchester line neared completion, the directors had to decide whether to risk using stationary steam engines instead, which would haul wagons along the lines by chain. They decided to hold a competition to test the reliability, speed and economy of the locomotives. The winner was *The Rocket*, designed by George Stephenson and his son Robert, which not only won but answered the directors' worries. It averaged 16 miles per hour (25 kilometres per hour) with a top speed of 29 mph, (about 46 kilometres) and completed the course without breaking down.

The Liverpool to Manchester Railway opened in September 1830 and was soon carrying 1200 passengers a day. Stagecoaches ran empty. It took longer for the railway to threaten the canal companies, but they had to reduce their charges to compete with the faster, more reliable railway. Not all passengers were enthusiastic. Thomas Creevey, a Whig MP, wrote after travelling at over 36 kilometres per hour,

> it is really flying and it is impossible to divest yourself of the notion of instant death to all … I am extremely glad indeed to have seen this miracle, and to have travelled in it … but, having done so, I am quite satisfied with my first achievement being my last.

The actress Fanny Kemble thought quite differently. She was entranced. George Stephenson took her on a trip shortly before the line opened. It was, she wrote,

> a magical machine, with its flying white breath and rhythmical, unvarying pace … I stood up, and with my bonnet off drank the air before me … When I closed my eyes this sensation of flying was quite delightful.

By 1832 thousands of other Britons shared her excitement. The landowners and politicians had escaped the political revolution they had feared. Instead they were being overtaken by a revolution few of them had expected, the railway revolution.

In 1825, as the first locomotive chugged along the Stockton to Darlington line, 'field and lanes were covered with elegantly-dressed females, and all descriptions of spectators. The bridges … lined with spectators cheering and waving their hats … Numerous horses, carriages, gigs, carts and other vehicles travelled along with the engine … and at one time the passengers by the engine had the pleasure of accompanying and cheering their brother passengers by the stagecoach, which passed alongside, and of observing the striking contrast exhibited by the power of the engine and of horses; the engine with her six hundred passengers and load, and the coach with four horses and only sixteen passengers'.

CHAPTER 6

The age of the railway

❖

The first shock of a great earthquake had, just at that period, rent the whole neighbourhood to its centre. Traces of its course were visible on every side. Houses were knocked down; streets broken through and stopped; deep pits and trenches dug in the ground; enormous heaps of earth and clay thrown up … Everywhere were bridges that led nowhere … fragments of unfinished walls and arches, and piles of scaffolding, and wildernesses of bricks … In short, the yet unfinished and unopened Railroad was in progress.

(above) A painting of Charles Dickens surrounded by characters from his novels. Dickens became the nation's favourite author in the nineteenth century, chiefly because of his genius as a story-teller but also because his 'gospel of kindliness, of brotherly love' attacked poverty and injustice.

(right) Excavating the railway at Camden in London, 1836.

By the time Charles Dickens's novel *Dombey and Son*, from which this extract comes, was published in 1848 every major town knew that scene. The 'pre-industrial world', said Dickens's fellow-novelist W.M.Thackeray in 1850, 'has passed into limbo and vanished … They have raised those railway embankments up, and shut off the old world that was behind them … it is gone'.

Stagecoaches vanished from the roads. The last bucketing stagecoach left London in 1846, Manchester in 1848. They lay around the countryside like beached whales, turned into hen coops or garden sheds. Coachmen, stablemen and grooms joined the railways as porters, clerks, messengers or engine drivers. By 1851 there were 65,000 railwaymen in jobs which had not existed thirty years earlier. In Dickens's view, railways created more than they destroyed: 'from the very core of this dire disorder', he wrote, 'the railroad trailed smoothly away, upon its mighty course of civilisation and improvement.'

Building the railways was often dangerous. This memorial in Otley, West Yorkshire, commemorates men who died building a tunnel. It is a reproduction of the tunnel entrance.

Cottonopolis: a city of ambition and poverty

The growing city of Manchester also caught the imagination of writers and politicians. Benjamin Disraeli, who was both, called Manchester a city of 'illumined factories taller than Egyptian obelisks'. Manchester, its skyline created by cotton mills and warehouses, was 'Cottonopolis', the capital of the Lancashire textile industry and the country's unofficial capital of trade.

In the 1820s, Manchester's medieval past still had influence. Shops, for example, were forbidden to challenge the centuries-old markets by selling meat or fish. In the 1840s Manchester's merchants and mill-owners determined to change the city. Public baths and parks were opened in 1846, then a public wash-house, and in 1852 new reservoirs and the first free municipal library in the country. But there was a darker side to Manchester. The German businessman and revolutionary, Friedrich Engels, described how Manchester's poorest labourers lived in the 1840s,

Heaps of refuse, offal and sickening filth are everywhere interspersed with pools of stagnant liquid … A horde of ragged women and children swarm about the streets and they are just as dirty as the pigs which wallow happily on the heaps of garbage and the pools of filth … on average twenty people live in each of these little houses … of two rooms, an attic and a cellar. One privy … is shared by about one hundred and twenty people.

In London in 1849 the journalist, Henry Mayhew, described an equally pitiful picture in the *Morning Chronicle*. He told of brickmakers and builders without work in winter, dockers pitched into poverty when

Sheffield in about 1850, painted by John McIntyre. Smoke from factory chimneys stands out above the town, but the artist seems more interested in the surrounding countryside. Perhaps he was saddened by the rapid growth of cities at this time.

'an ill wind' kept ships out of port. The poor lived on potatoes, condensed milk, tea made from tea-leaves already used in more prosperous kitchens, white bread made from flour mixed with chalk, jam mixed with copper or turnips. Their water frequently came from 'the common sewer which stagnates full [of] dead fish, cats and dogs'.

Yet the greatest nightmare for the poor was the workhouse. In 1834 the Whig government changed the Poor Law, stopping the payment of cash relief to the unemployed and the old who lived in their own homes. Now, in order to receive help or 'relief' they had to enter workhouses where conditions 'shall not be made as eligible [desirable] as the situation of the independent labourer of the lowest class'. Families were separated, made to feel like criminals and wear workhouse clothes.

This 'cruel, illegal' law, said the Huddersfield Anti-Poor Law Committee, was intended 'to lower wages and punish poverty as a crime'. Fear of the workhouse drove parents, desperate for work, to leave their babies with 'baby-farmers' who kept them half-starved, drugged and watched over by three-year-olds.

The People's Charter

In the late 1830s anger at the new workhouses in the north provoked demonstrations. These were often addressed by an Irishman, who had been an MP, Feargus O'Connor. He started a newspaper, the *Northern Star*, in 1838 in which he railed against the workhouses and argued for the vote for working class people. In London in 1836 William Lovett, a

The Six Points
OF THE
PEOPLE'S
CHARTER.

1. A VOTE for every man twenty-one years of age, of sound mind, and not undergoing punishment for crime.

2. THE BALLOT.—To protect the elector in the exercise of his vote.

3. No PROPERTY QUALIFICATION for Members of Parliament —thus enabling the constituencies to return the man of their choice, be he rich or poor.

4. PAYMENT OF MEMBERS, thus enabling an honest trades-man, working man, or other person, to serve a constituency, when taken from his business to attend to the interests of the country.

5. EQUAL CONSTITUENCIES, securing the same amount of representation for the same number of electors, instead of allowing small constituencies to swamp the votes of large ones.

6. ANNUAL PARLIAMENTS, thus presenting the most effectual check to bribery and intimidation, since though a constituency might be bought once in seven years (even with the ballot), no purse could buy a constituency (under a system of universal suffrage) in each ensuing twelvemonth; and since members, when elected for a year only, would not be able to defy and betray their constituents as now.

(above) The Six Points of the People's Charter.

(below) In 1839, 5000 Chartists demonstrated in Newport. 24 were killed by soldiers.

cabinet-maker, started the London Working Men's Association. Lovett was less fiery than O'Connor, and wanted to persuade Parliament that political reform was needed. He drew up the *Six Points of the People's Charter* which was printed on handbills such as the one on this page. In 1838 O'Connor and Lovett met at a huge meeting in Birmingham to form the Chartist movement. Chartist rallies and meetings all over the country demanded that Parliament agree to the 'Six Points'.

Support for Chartism was wide-spread. The 1832 Reform Act had not ended demands for reform. Robert Lowery, a Newcastle Chartist, wrote that the arguments over the Act,

> developed thought among the more reflecting, and began discussion on the principles of government and of national prosperity. It produced thinkers in every class, and more especially the working classes.

In the 1830s and 1840s over eighty Political Unions and Chartist Associations were founded for women alone. In 1836 the Female Political Union of Newcastle explained why they wanted political reform,

> For years we have struggled to maintain our homes in comfort, such as our hearts told us should greet our husbands after their fatiguing labours. Year after year have passed away, and … the working men who form the millions, the strength and wealth of the country, are left without [outside] the pale of the Constitution.

In 1839 and 1842 Chartists carried huge petitions of signatures to Parliament, but ministers refused to accept them. Demonst-rations followed, many of them violent, but troops broke them up. The Newport Rising convinced some politicians that the Welsh language was a cause of revolt. English commissioners were sent to report on Welsh education, and their report condemned the use of Welsh in schools as 'backward'. The report was known as 'The Treachery of the Blue Books'.

Self-help or government help?

Both political parties, Whigs and Conservatives, opposed the Chartists' demands. The Conservatives were the old Tories, revived by Peel in the 1830s after they had been shattered by the defeat over the Great Reform Act. They were still cautious about any reform, believing that government should not intervene in people's lives. This attitude was summed up by Samuel Smiles in his book *Self Help*, published in 1857. 'Whatever is done for men takes away the stimulus of doing for themselves', he wrote. 'Heaven helps those who help themselves.'

The Whigs (who stayed in power between 1830 and 1852 except for the years between 1834–35 and 1841–46 when Peel's Conservatives were in government) were slightly more inclined to intervene, often persuaded by campaigners or crises. In 1833, for example, Lord Shaftesbury and others persuaded MPs to ban the employment of children under nine in factories, and cut the working day for those under eighteen to twelve hours. In the same year, just a month after the death of the anti-slavery campaigner and MP, William Wilberforce, slavery was abolished throughout the British Empire from January 1834.

In 1833 reformers also persuaded the Whigs to make a grant of £20,000 to help religious societies build schools for the poor. By 1862 the grant had risen to £150,000 but concern at the size of the grant led to a system of 'payment by results'. The amount of money a school received depended on how many pupils attended regularly and passed tests set by visiting inspectors. This in turn led to teachers teaching pupils to learn the answers to tests by rote (by heart). The result, according to the school inspector Matthew Arnold, was that 'teaching … has certainly fallen off in intelligence, spirit and inventivenesss … everyone is prone to rely too much on mechanical processes and too little on intelligence'. Even so, more children were learning to read and write, although schooling was not compulsory.

There were also arguments over public health. In 1848 *The Times* published this letter,

> Sur, May we beg and beseech your proteckshion… We live in muck and filthe. We aint got no privez, no dust bins, no water supplies, no drain or suer in the whole place … We al of us suffer and numbers are ill and if the Cholera comes lord help us.

The cholera came, and in 1848 alone killed 53,000 people. The epidemic persuaded Parliament to pass a Public Health Act, allowing towns with the highest death rates to set up Boards of Health to improve water supplies and build sewage systems. However, many politicians thought that the government's Board of Health in London and its secretary, Edwin Chadwick, had been given too much power. In 1854 *The Times* ageed: 'we prefer to take our chance of cholera and the rest than be bullied into health. There is nothing a man hates so much as being cleaned against his will'.

A cartoon from 1849, suggesting one way to avoid the terrible and unhealthy smells in the streets of the city.

Famine in Ireland

In the 1840s another group of campaigning politicians and industrialists, based in Manchester, challenged the government when they created the Anti-Corn Law League. They wanted to end import duties on corn (see page 298). Their aim was cheap bread for all but the Conservative landowners resisted, fearing ruin if the Corn Laws were repealed.

The issue was settled when in 1845 the Irish potato crop was struck by blight. The population, dependent on potatoes for their food and livelihood, watched helpless as fields turned into 'masses of putrid slime'. Starvation stared them in the face. Prime Minister Peel proposed abolishing the Corn Laws to allow cheap maize into Ireland, but most Conservatives saw this as a threat to English agriculture and profits. Peel rounded on his colleagues,

> Good God! are you to sit in cabinet and consider and calculate how much diarrhoea and bloody flux and dysentery a people can bear before it becomes necessary for you to provide them with food?

At last, in 1846 Peel won the argument. The Corn Laws were abolished, but only with the help of opposition MPs. The Commons debate split the Conservatives and forced Peel's resignation. But repeal came too late to save the 800,000 people who died in Ireland. Over the next twenty-five years nearly three million people emigrated from Ireland, mainly to the United States.

This illustration showing half-starved children searching for potatoes in Ireland appeared in the Illustrated London News *in December 1849.*

A magistrate from Cork wrote to The Times *describing the hovels in Skibbereen in County Cork: 'In the first, six famished and ghastly skeletons ... I approached with horror, and found by a low moaning that they were alive – they were in fever, four children, a woman and what had once been a man. ... In a few minutes I was surrounded by at least 200 of such phantoms, such frightful spectres as no words can describe.'*

1848: the last petition

Two years later, in 1848, the fear of revolution returned to England. Londoners watched as the Duke of Wellington, still the army's Commander in Chief, placed cannon on London's bridges. Ten thousand soldiers stood by in readiness. The 'dangerous classes' were marching again. The cause of political reform had been kept alive by Chartism, as Benjamin Watson, a Halifax Chartist, later remembered,

> Amongst combers, handloom weavers, and others politics was the chief topic. The *Northern Star* was their principal paper, and it was a common practice, particularly in villages, to meet at friends' houses to read the paper and talk over political matters ... We were only waiting for the time to come again.

In 1848 cholera struck again, and in Europe revolutions flared. Palmerston called these a 'political earthquake … thrones shaken, shattered, levelled', but in Britain there was no rebellion. A Chartist committee, chaired by William Cuffay, a black journeyman tailor and an active Chartist since 1839 organized another petition to Parliament. Several thousands gathered to present this 'monster petition' to Parliament, but it held only two million signatures, far fewer than the five million which their leaders claimed and many were forged, including those of Queen Victoria, Peel and Wellington, who was apparently so enthusiastic for the Charter that he had signed seventeen times!

The Chartists' failure seemed to show that discontent was fading. Many people were finding jobs in new industries. Better food supplies meant that bad harvests caused less suffering. By the 1850s the development of local police forces meant that governments did not have to rely on the much-resented soldiers.

A photograph of the Great Chartist Meeting on Kennington Common, 10 April 1848. Cameras were developed in the 1830s and the first book illustrated with photographs was published in 1841. Photography created a new source of evidence for historians, but remained black and white until the mid-twentieth-century.

Protecting British trade

No one symbolized this confident and ambitious Britain more than Lord Palmerston, the Whig Foreign Secretary for fifteen of the years between 1830 and 1852. Protecting Britain's trade and colonies were his main concerns. In 1838 Chinese officials tried to stop British merchants selling opium in their country, by seizing every ounce of the drug owned by British traders in the Chinese port of Canton. The Imperial Commissioner wrote to the young Queen Victoria,

> So long as you tempt the people of China to buy it [opium] you will be showing yourselves careful of your own lives but careless, in your greed for gain, of the harm you do to others.

more than ten years later, the start of the nursing profession for trained staff. Russell's reports also led to a parliamentary enquiry into the management of the war. As a result the Prime Minister, Lord Aberdeen, resigned. He was replaced by Palmerston, the one politician in whom people had confidence.

In 1857 Palmerston faced another crisis, this time in India itself, where rebellion broke out sparked off by Indian soldiers of the East Indian Company who mutinied, slaughtering British soldiers and their families. The rebellion might have been successful if it had not been for 'that cursed wire', as one nationalist called the electric telegraph, which chattered out warnings and orders. British troops regained control but not before an increase in violence by large numbers of mutineers, as well as outbreaks of revenge atrocities by British troops.

Palmerston decided that it was time for the government to take over the administration of India, which until then had been in the hands of the East India Company. British district officers, police officers and engineers imposed what they saw as the benefits of European life: systems of law and regular taxation, railways, canals and irrigation schemes. In fact they weakened the Indian way of life. The British demand for plantation crops and the spread of British-made goods damaged Indian village agriculture and handicraft industries.

'Wealth is ... within reach of all'

Palmerston was as confident about Britain's economic power as he was about her overseas policies. In 1865 he told his audience at the South London Industrial Exhibition,

> Wealth is, to a certain extent, within reach of all...you are competitors for prizes...you will by systematic industry, raise yourselves in the social system of the country – you will acquire honour and respect for yourselves and your families ... Go on, ladies and gentlemen, and prosper.

In the 1850s and 1860s Britain's economy was expanding as fast as it ever did during the nineteenth century. There were new opportunities in every branch of work. The fast-growing population needed houses, railways needed stations and tunnels, creating work for builders, brickmakers, painters. Steelworkers, engineers and colliers were needed to supply the railways with tracks, engines and fuel. New markets in South America and Africa created more work for dock labourers, warehousemen and seamen. Every employer needed clerks, to tally wages, sales and purchases, copy wills or bills of sale for lawyers, and complete the birth, marriage and death certificates required by law after 1838. Banks and the increasing number of small shops needed cashiers.

Clerks, teachers, shopkeepers and others in middle-class jobs certainly had more money to spend. Some employed servants, a sure way of showing their neighbours that they were prospering. In 1851 about

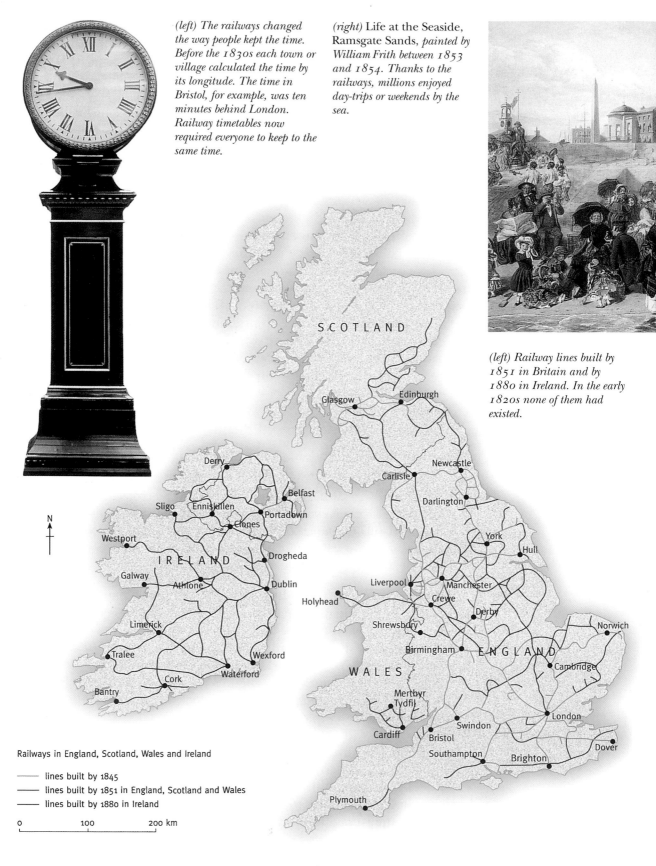

(left) The railways changed the way people kept the time. Before the 1830s each town or village calculated the time by its longitude. The time in Bristol, for example, was ten minutes behind London. Railway timetables now required everyone to keep to the same time.

(right) Life at the Seaside, Ramsgate Sands, *painted by William Frith between 1853 and 1854. Thanks to the railways, millions enjoyed day-trips or weekends by the sea.*

(left) Railway lines built by 1851 in Britain and by 1880 in Ireland. In the early 1820s none of them had existed.

N

SCOTLAND

Glasgow   Edinburgh

Newcastle
Carlisle
Darlington
York
Hull

Derry
Belfast
Sligo   Enniskillen
Portadown
Clones
Westport
IRELAND   Drogheda
Galway   Athlone   Dublin
Holyhead   Liverpool   Manchester
Crewe   Derby
Limerick   Shrewsbury   Norwich
Tralee   Wexford   Birmingham   ENGLAND
Cork   Waterford   WALES   Cambridge
Bantry   Merthyr Tydfil   London
Cardiff   Swindon
Bristol   Dover
Southampton   Brighton
Plymouth

Railways in England, Scotland, Wales and Ireland

—— lines built by 1845
—— lines built by 1851 in England, Scotland and Wales
—— lines built by 1880 in Ireland

0   100   200 km

850,000 people had work as servants (750,000 of them women). By 1871 this number had soared to 1,329,000 (including 1.2 million women).

The railways, always the railways, helped them spend more. Every morning, as the *Railway News* noted in 1864, 'we see … the supply of the great London markets rapidly unloaded by these night trains; fish, flesh and food, Aylesbury butter and dairy-fed pork, apples, cabbages and cucumber'. Fresh food and milk were new for most town-dwellers. So too were holidays, thanks to the 'Napoleon of Excursions', Thomas Cook.

Cook made his fortune by arranging railway excursions. The first of these, in 1841, from Leicester to Loughborough, was an outing for members of the temperance movement, all strong opponents of the 'demon drink' and for drinkers, attracted out of taverns by the adventure. Cook, a devout Baptist, always regarded travel as 'a form of missionary enterprise against the demoralizing influences of the bottle', made possible only by the railway. By 1845 railway excursions, to horse-races, concerts or even public executions, were all the rage.

The Crystal Palace, which housed the Great Exhibition, was designed and built by Joseph Paxton, who began his career as the superintendent of the Duke of Devonshire's gardens. He based his design on the huge glasshouses on the duke's estate. Most of the parts were made separately then put together on the site. It was over 540 metres long, 117 metres wide and 22 metres high. Paxton later designed public parks and became an MP – the very model of a successful Victorian.

Cook's name first caught the public eye at the Great Exhibition of 1851. The Great Exhibition of the Works of Industry of All Nations lived up to its name, exhibiting 10,000 objects from every part of the world. But it was dominated by British manufacturers, and celebrated British success as the organizers, including Prince Albert, intended.

Six million tickets were sold and people travelled by train from every part of Britain on cheap excursions. Whole factories closed for their visit to London. Entire villages saved up to make the journey together. Mary Collinack, aged 85, walked to the Exhibition from Penzance. The Great Exhibition was the ideal Victorian entertainment, respectable, educational, 'improving'. 'Even idleness is eager now', wrote the novelist George Eliot, 'eager for amusement; prone [inclined] to excursion trains,

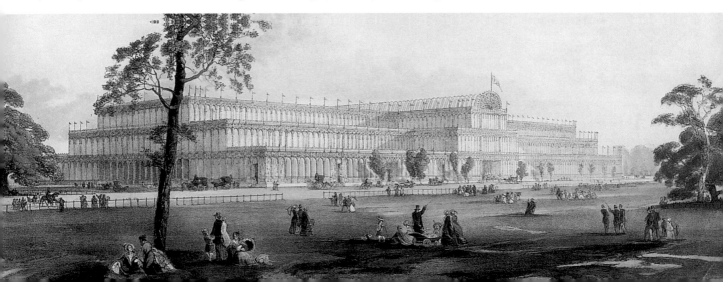

During the 1850s craft-workers such as engineers and carpenters developed powerful trades unions, which negotiated shorter working hours and higher wages. These 'aristocrats of labour' could afford the subscriptions to unions, and weekly payments to Friendly Societies for insurance against sickness or unemployment. Unskilled workers simply could not afford these payments, and were not included in the early unions. This is a certificate of 1852 for members of the Amalgamated Society of Engineers, Machinists, Millwrights, Smiths and Patternmakers.

art-museums, periodical literature, and exciting novels; prone even to scientific theorizing, and cursory [quick] peeps through microscopes'.

Amid this prosperity the anger of the rioters had faded, but the demand for more political reform had not. The Chartists' ideas lived on, especially among members of the new trades unions of skilled workers, who argued for the right to a say in how the country was governed. Henry Mayhew recorded in 1861 that,

The artisans are almost to a man red-hot politicians. They are sufficiently educated and thoughtful to have a sense of their importance in the State ... The political character and sentiments of the working classes appear to me to be a distinctive feature of the age.

Even within the Liberal government, whose leading figures were drawn from the aristocracy, younger men were pressing for new approaches, or 'reforms' as they called them. According to Palmerston, who was Prime Minister until he died in 1865, his Chancellor, W.E.Gladstone, was 'charged to the muzzle with all sorts of schemes of all sorts of reforms'. Palmerston steadfastly resisted Gladstone's schemes, but he expected that, in the future, 'Gladstone will soon have it all his own way and whenever he gets my place we shall have strange days'.

Reformers were spurred on in their desire for change by the rapid changes in the world around them, such as those in science and engineering. Many believed, like the Poet Laureate, Alfred Lord Tennyson, that change itself was a good thing,

For I dipt into the future, far as human eye could see,
Saw the Vision of the world and all the wonder that would be;
Not in vain the distance beacons. Forward, forward let us rage.
Let the great world spin forever down the ringing grooves of change.

CHAPTER 7
Victorian triumph and decline

❖

In 1864 a notice appeared on the gates of Buckingham Palace in London. It read, 'These commanding premises to be let or sold, in consequence of the late occupant's declining business'. Queen Victoria was not dead but she had disappeared from public view since the death of her husband Prince Albert in 1861. In her own words, she 'would have followed [Albert] barefoot all over the world'. Now she was a 'poor broken-hearted widow' and mother of eight, doomed to a 'pleasureless, dreary life'. In the 1860s, as 'the widow of Windsor' hid herself from her subjects, the monarchy became deeply unpopular. Over eighty republican clubs were founded prompting the political journalist, Walter Bagehot, to write, ' the queen has done

In 1877 Queen Victoria was proclaimed Empress of India. Although she ruled the largest empire in history, with a quarter of the world's population and nearly a quarter of its land, royal power was declining. For example, although Victoria detested Gladstone she could not prevent him becoming Prime Minister four times between 1868 and his retirement in 1894, aged 85. She could influence the choice of Cabinet members, but she had much less influence than George III in the 1770s.

almost as much to injure the popularity of the monarchy as the most unworthy of her predecessors'.

Victoria's unpopularity continued for nearly twenty years until, gradually, she was persuaded out of her seclusion by advisers, in particular Benjamin Disraeli, who was the Conservative Prime Minister between 1874 and 1880. Victoria's Golden Jubilee in 1887 confirmed the public's new enthusiasm for the monarchy. The queen's portrait was emblazoned on biscuit tins and pottery – mugs, jugs, bowls and plates – and her praises were sung in the new popular magazines. The Diamond Jubilee in 1897 saw the revival of British ceremonial, adorned by the music of Edward Elgar who wrote his *Imperial March* the same year. Detailed planning of the events set a standard for the future, a far cry from the wedding of the Prince of Wales in 1863 when Lord Robert Cecil, later Marquis of Salisbury and Prime Minister, had commented that, 'some nations have a gift for ceremonial … In England the case is exactly the reverse'.

Victoria's long life enabled her to survive republican ideas and become a symbol of national pride and imperial strength, just at the time when other nations were rivalling Britain's economic strength. In the harsh world of trade and industrial development, Britain's days of dominance were nearly over.

One of the few faces known to most Victorians was that of W.G.Grace. He was the greatest cricketer of the age and dominated the sport for over thirty years. He made his debut for an All-England XI aged fifteen, and last played for England aged 51. When Grace was playing admission charges were often doubled. Although he was a doctor and supposedly an amateur, Grace was handsomely paid for playing cricket. Between 1873 and 1874 he received £1500 for a tour of Australia. The professionals in the side were paid £170. So many people were eager to see him that he had to play in every match of the tour!

At the match and in the shops

Victorians in steady jobs in the 1880s and 1890s did not notice any decline in their prosperity. Workers enjoyed four Bank Holidays, introduced in 1871, and many had free Saturday afternoons when men flocked to watch Football League matches or cricket's County Championship. Professional sport began to be played in towns where entrance charges from the crowds were large enough to pay the players' wages. Football flourished because spectators had free time and railways could carry teams and supporters to away matches; newspapers fanned the enthusiasm with reports of matches and league tables.

Enthusiasm for team games had been encouraged in the public schools. As late as 1882 old boys from Eton School beat Blackburn Rovers in the F.A. Cup Final after a Blackburn forward, according to the *Blackburn Times*, 'shot the leather over the bar of the Etonian citadel'. However, Rovers went on to win the Cup three years running, from 1884 to 1886 and, when the Football League was formed in 1888, its twelve pioneer clubs came from northern and midland industrial towns, among them Preston, Accrington and Nottingham.

PLAYER'S CIGARETTES

LADY CYCLIST WEARING
DIVIDED SKIRT

A lady cyclist, on a cigarette card of the late 1890s.

Michael Marks's Penny Bazaar, founded in Leeds Market in 1884, later to grow into Marks and Spencer. This stall is in Huddersfield Market, where Marks & Spencer traded between 1894 and 1925. Markets were beginning to lose customers to the new chain stores, such as Freeman, Hardy and Willis who sold factory-made shoes throughout the country from the 1870s. New kinds of goods were now appearing in the shops. In the 1870s chewing gum, toilet rolls, jeans and milk chocolate were sold for the first time.

As professional sports blossomed, women struggled to take part. The Original English Lady Cricketers played in 1890 under assumed names, for fear of derision. Women who played tennis did so in 'a cream merino bodice with long sleeves edged with embroidery; skirt with deep kilting, over it an old-gold silk blouse tunic with short wide sleeves and square neck' and a straw hat. Lottie Dod won the Wimbledon singles in 1887 at the age of fifteen, wearing a calf-length dress that would have been unacceptably short on anyone older.

It was even difficult for women to win acceptance as cyclists. John Dunlop's invention of the pneumatic tyre in Belfast in 1888 started a cycling craze. One enthusiast, Louise Jeye, saw it as 'a new dawn, a dawn of emancipation [freedom]… free to wheel, free to spin out into the glorious countryside, unhampered by chaperon or, even more dispiriting, male admirer'. However, the magazine *Lady's Realm* denounced female cyclists as lacking 'the faintest remnant of that sweet spirit of allurement [temptation] which … is woman's supreme attraction'. Passers-by jeered at women cyclists, and in 1899 one was struck by a meat-hook thrown by a bystander.

MARKS & SPENCER L⁰

REGISTERED OFFICE & WAREHOUSE
DERBY ST — CHEETHAM.

With the population growing from 27.4 million in 1851 to 41.4 million in 1901 there was a huge market for pioneers of chain stores like Jesse Boot and Thomas Lipton. Stores mailed catalogues and delivered orders over long distances to those who could afford their prices. In the High Street, wealthier customers could shop in the new department stores. One enthusiastic shopper wrote that,

> Our 'Stores' becomes at once a place for one to take one's friends and to meet one's friends; a fashionable resort, a lounge, an art gallery, a bazaar and a delightful promenade.

The 'maniac' versus 'the gamester'

All these improvements did not stop demands for political reform. When Palmerston died in 1865, William Gladstone, his successor as leader of the Liberals (as the Whigs were now known) was determined to give the vote to working men. An alliance between his party and skilled workers could keep it in power for many years and, at the same time, carried no risk of social revolution.

(right) 'If you boiled Gladstone you would not find an ounce of fun in him', said Lady Palmerston. His hobbies were tree-felling and translating hymns into Latin, yet crowds flocked to see him during political campaigns when his train stopped in town or country. Newspapers printed his speeches in full, even though they sometimes lasted three or four hours!

(far right) Benjamin Disraeli, later Lord Beaconsfield. Disraeli was defeated in three elections before he became an MP in 1837, aged 33. Despite his family's wealth and his fame as a novelist, his Jewish background made him an outsider. His appearance shocked the sober politicians of the 1830s. A contemporary described how he wore, 'a black velvet coat lined with satin, purple trousers with a gold band running down the outside seam, a scarlet waistcoat, long lace ruffles falling down to the tips of his fingers … and long black ringlets rippling down upon his shoulders'.

The Conservative politician, Benjamin Disraeli, was determined to prevent Gladstone winning the support of new voters. His aim, he said, was simply to 'dish the Whigs!' Disraeli made an alliance with rebel Liberals who disliked Gladstone's proposals. Together they out-voted Gladstone in Parliament, destroying his moderate plans. Then, astonishingly, the new government led by Disraeli and Derby (the leader of the Conservative party), introduced their own scheme, which was more radical than Gladstone's! Their Reform Act of 1867 gave the vote to an additional one million working men. This doubled the number of voters to sixteen per cent of all adults.

The rivalry between Gladstone and Disraeli did not cool. To Disraeli, Gladstone was 'that unprincipled maniac' and 'a vindictive fiend'. Gladstone claimed that Disraeli's policies brought 'suffering, discredit and dishonour' to Britain. As Prime Minister (for the first time in 1868–1874 and the second in 1880–1885) Gladstone reformed the Civil Service, so that civil servants were recruited only after passing examinations, rather than because they were related to influential people. Secret ballots, which had earlier been a demand of the Chartists, were introduced at elections after 1872, ending the use of bribery and threats. Working men in rural areas were given the vote in the Third Reform Act of 1884, which increased the electorate to twenty-nine per cent of adults.

In 1870 Gladstone's government set up School Boards throughout the country. The people on these Boards had to ensure that new schools were built wherever they were needed. For the first time a government took responsibility for the spread of education, rather than only giving grants to religious societies to provide schools. This change was partly the result of the 1867 Reform Act. 'From the moment you entrust the masses with power, their education becomes an imperative necessity', said the Liberal politician, Robert Lowe. In February 1870 W.E. Forster, the MP behind the education reforms, gave Parliament other reasons for the government's actions,

> We must not delay…Upon the speedy provision of elementary education depends our industrial prosperity. It is of no use trying to give technical teaching to our artisans without elementary education … if we leave our workfolk any longer unskilled … they will become over-matched in the competition of the world.

In 1880 schooling was made compulsory between the ages of five and thirteen, although pupils who reached a certain standard of work could leave earlier. One result was that by 1900 only five per cent of the population could neither read nor write, compared with thirty per cent of men and forty per cent of women in 1850.

Disraeli's motives for reform were not straightforward. To the Marquess of Salisbury, a later Conservative leader, he seemed at times 'a mere political gamester', interested only in personal ambition. However as a young novelist Disraeli had, in one of his novels, *Sybil*, published in 1845, criticized the great divide in Britain between the 'Two Nations' of rich and poor. As Prime Minister in 1874 he returned to those ideals, announcing that, 'the great object is to be practical … Pure air, pure water, the inspection of unhealthy habitations, the adulteration of food … the first consideration of a Minister should be the health of the people'. He also hoped that such practical reforms would win votes.

In 1875 Disraeli kept his word. His Public Health Act made local authorities purify water supplies, provide sewage systems and appoint Medical Officers of Health to oversee improvements. This reform, in conjunction with medical advances such as Louis Pasteur's discovery that bacteria caused diseases and Robert Koch's development of Jenner's work with vaccinations, finally deposed 'King

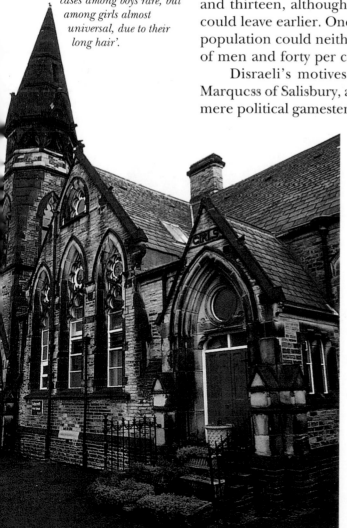

The 1870 Education Act said that local School Boards could raise taxes to build schools in areas where there were not enough school places. By 1900, 2500 had been built in England and Wales. This Board School was built in Bradford. The Board Schools did have a great effect. One headmaster noted that between 1882 and 1900 boys had become 'much more docile; insubordination, then endemic, now almost unknown … Truancy almost extinct … Personal cleanliness greatly improved; verminous cases among boys rare, but among girls almost universal, due to their long hair'.

Cholera' and the other epidemic diseases that had rampaged out of control for so long. The death-rate began to fall. In 1871 the average life expectancy was still below forty-five. By 1911 life expectancy for men had risen to fifty, for women to fifty-five. Women in particular benefited from the widespread use of antiseptics in hospitals and homes, which cut the death-toll among new mothers.

Poverty and the growth of socialism

Despite these improvements, the politicians remained reluctant to enforce change. 'Permissive legislation is the character of a free people', said Disraeli, 'in a free country...you must trust to persuasion and example'. Gladstone for once agreed. 'If the government takes into its hand that which a man ought to do for himself', he said, 'it will inflict upon him greater mischiefs than all the benefits he will have received'.

But evidence was growing to show that life for the very poor remained hard, especially for the large numbers of households where neither man nor woman had regular work. Individuals set up new organizations to try to remedy these problems. Thomas Barnardo set up his home for destitute boys in 1870, William and Catherine Booth formed the Salvation Army in 1878, and the National Society for the Prevention of Cruelty to Children (NSPCC) was established in 1884.

Systematic evidence of how the very poor were living came from Charles Booth's survey of *The Life and Labour of the People in London*, published in seventeen volumes between 1889 and 1902. Booth was a shipping magnate, who at first could not believe the descriptions he heard of extreme poverty. He decided to see for himself and, horrified, discovered that as many as a third of Londoners lived in poverty.

Unskilled workers banded together in trade unions, to defend themselves against employers eager to cut wages. They demanded better wages, safer places to work and shorter hours. Before the late 1880s this kind of organization had been impossible. Those looking for work were often rivals. The dockers' leader Ben Tillett described how 'men ravening for food fought like madmen for the ticket [for work] ... Coats,

'Guinea Graves' in Becket Street Cemetery in Leeds. These are not the graves of the very poor because they were buried in unmarked graves. The families of these people scraped together a guinea (£1.05) to have the name inscribed on the tombstone, next to those of others who were buried the same way in a common grave. So closely packed were the burials that these stones have names on both sides.

Farmworkers finally built their National Agricultural Labourers' Union in 1872, thanks to the drive of Joseph Arch, but they suffered greatly when bad harvests led to the 'Great Depression' of the 1870s and 1880s. Cheap corn flooded in from America, refrigerated ships brought meat from New Zealand and Argentina, and sheep-farmers faced competition from Australian wool. The number of agricultural workers fell steadily as people left the countryside for the towns, seeking steady work.

The wives and children of striking dockers in 1889. Public donations helped the dockers draw strike pay and paid for food for their families.

A survey in 1900 showed that ten-year-old boys from families such as these were, on average, five inches shorter than ten-year-old boys from wealthy families in private schools.

flesh, and even ears, were torn off, men crushed to death in the struggle'. Two strikes showed the way forward.

In 1888 the match girls at Bryant and May's match factory in London went on strike. They were organized by a journalist, Annie Besant, who was shocked when she found that girls there worked ten hours a day, were fined and beaten. The phosphorus used on the matches gave them 'phossy-jaw', a disease which rotted their jaw-bones. After a strike lasting three weeks their working conditions improved. The following year Ben Tillett and John Burns led the London dockers in a five-week strike for an extra penny on top of their fivepence an hour. Encouraged by these victories, other workers organized unions.

In 1892 a Lanarkshire miner from Scotland gave another shock to traditional politics. James

Keir Hardie was elected to Parliament as Independent Labour member for West Ham, in London. Hardie was a socialist, believing that industries should be owned by the people for the benefit of all, and that the rich should be taxed to support the poor. Although Hardie only held his seat for three years, in 1900 trade unions and socialists combined to form the Labour Representation Committee (LRC), and pledged to fight to elect working men to Parliament. Two LRC candidates were elected in 1900, one of whom was Keir Hardie, at Merthyr Tydfil.

The LRC's success was limited, but it was envied by those campaigning for votes for women. After 1867, Parliament almost yearly debated a bill to give women the vote. Each time the bill was defeated, but the campaign drew more support. In 1867 Lydia Becker founded the Manchester Women's Suffrage Committee and soon Suffrage Societies flourished in many towns. Their members were mainly middle-class women educated in the girls' High Schools, which were set up in increasing numbers from the 1850s.

They made some progress. In 1873 divorced women won the right to custody of their children. All women gained the legal right to keep their property and income after marriage, instead of it being automatically owned by their husbands.

Nationally women had been able to vote for Poor Law Guardians since 1834, for School Boards from 1870 and for local councils from 1888. Despite the difficulties, the determined campaign by women for the right to vote for Members of Parliament continued. In 1897, 500 Suffrage Societies joined together to form the National Union of Women's Suffrage Societies. It was headed by Millicent Fawcett.

The disunited kingdom?

In 1887 celebrations throughout Britain marked Queen Victoria's Golden Jubilee. Yet that same year Welsh nationalists founded Cymru Fydd ('Young Wales'), whose aim was a Welsh parliament with its own ministers. The previous year a Scottish Home Rule Association had been formed and a series of campaigns, both violent and peaceful, had led Gladstone to decide that Ireland should have Home Rule and its own parliament. 'It certainly does look', wrote the Conservative Home Secretary, 'as though the

Each step forward for women was the result of a hard fight by individuals. When Elizabeth Garrett, shown here, attended medical lectures at the Middlesex Hospital, in London, in 1861, male students protested at 'an outrage to our natural instincts' and Miss Garrett had to study privately. In

1870 women were accepted as students in medical schools at Edinburgh and at London in 1878. Most men and many women agreed with the scientist T.H. Huxley that, 'in every excellent characteristic, whether mental or physical, the average woman is inferior to the average man'.

A monument to William Wallace who led Scottish resistance to Edward I. It was erected in Stirling in 1869, a sign of growing pride in Scotland's history of independence, including Wallace's victory at Stirling Bridge in 1297.

Scots remembered their centuries of independence with pride, and many of them also wanted a Scottish Church which was theirs. They were also very conscious of the contribution their country had made to the expansion of the British economy and to the creation of a worldwide empire.

spirit of nationality, which has united Germany and Italy, were operating to disintegrate [break up] this country'.

In fact in Wales and Scotland the Home Rule movements won little practical support, although the people of both countries were proud of being Welsh or Scots, rather than British. In 1900 about half the Welsh people still spoke their native language, despite efforts to stamp it out in schools following 'The Treachery of the Blue Books' in 1847. Some Welsh politicians wanted to separate the Church in Wales from the Church of England, to direct more money to Welsh chapels.

In Ireland, nationalism fed on bitter memories. James Lalor, a young nationalist, wrote in 1848 about the Great Famine (see page 313). It had caused hundreds of thousands of deaths and started the great overseas migration of Irish people, which was to continue into the next century. Lalor believed that,

> A people, whose lands and lives are ... in the keeping and custody of others instead of their own, are not in a position of common safety. Had the people of Ireland been the landlords of Ireland, not a single human creature would have died of hunger.

The only answer for Lalor and other Nationalists was Home Rule, the return of Dublin's parliament and the end of the union with Britain.

In the 1870s and 1880s British politicians swung between trying to suppress nationalistic campaigns and trying to remove laws which made life hard for the Catholics who made up the mass of the population. Led by Gladstone, the Liberals passed laws which guaranteed fair rents for tenant farmers and gave them protection from unfair evictions from their homes by landlords, most of whom were Protestant. Catholics no longer had to pay tithes to the Protestant Church of Ireland.

However, instead of withering, demands for Home Rule grew. The Home Rulers' chance came after the 1884 Reform Act, which gave many Catholic farmers the vote. The following year they elected eighty-six MPs, who supported Home Rule. Charles Stuart Parnell was their leader in the Commons, where the group held the balance of power between the Conservatives and Liberals. Gladstone needed the Home Rulers' support to out-vote the Conservatives on other matters. Parnell's price was Home Rule for Ireland. Gladstone, by now persuaded of the need for Home Rule, agreed.

Their plans sparked three weeks of rioting and thirty-two deaths in Ulster, where the Protestant majority was determined to maintain the union with Britain, even to the point of taking up arms. A leading Conservative, Lord Randolph Churchill, urged them on, with the slogan 'Ulster will fight and Ulster will be right'. When MPs came to vote on Gladstone's Home Rule Bill, the Conservatives voted to keep the Union and won the support of a group of rebel Liberals, headed by Joseph Chamberlain. Together they defeated Gladstone. They did so again in 1893. Home Rule split the Liberals. Chamberlain's rebels joined the Conservatives to form the 'Conservative and Unionist Party'.

A street in the town of Youghal in Ireland in 1895. The houses were mostly rented from an absent landlord.

Although it seemed as if the Home Rule demand had been destroyed, Irish nationalism was anything but dead. There was increased interest in Ireland's Celtic and Gaelic past, in the Gaelic language and sports, music and theatre. The Gaelic Athletic Association was founded 'for the preservation and cultivation of our national pastimes'. By 1900 there were over 400 Gaelic football and hurling clubs. Britain was still united, but 1886 had drawn the lines of future conflict. It was now clear that the Ulster Protestants would fight any further plans for Home Rule.

Have you heard the talk of foreign pow'rs?

In the 1870s and 1880s pride in the British Empire was at its height. When Russia again threatened the trading routes to India in 1878 crowds raised the roofs of music halls with songs such as this:

> We don't want to fight, but by jingo if we do,
> We've got the ships, we've got the men, we've got the money too.
> We've fought the Bear before, and while we're Britons true,
> The Russians shall not have Constantinople.

However, beneath this bravado lurked fears of rivalries and competition unknown since 1815. Another music hall song asked,

Have you heard the talk of foreign pow'rs
Building ships increasingly?
Do you know they watch this isle of ours?
Watch their chance unceasingly? …

Faced by her three increasingly powerful rivals, France, Germany and Russia, Britain set about planning the safety of her empire. Politicians were often reluctant colonizers but they knew that if Britain did not take part in the 'Scramble for Africa' her rivals would seize their chance. One conquest almost always led to another. A fast route to India was created by building the Suez Canal in Egypt, connecting the Mediterranean Sea with the Red Sea. It was opened in 1869 and Britain, needing to dominate that route, first took control of Egypt and then occupied the Sudan. Still British ministers were wary. What if France won control of the head-waters of the Nile, threatening the Sudan? Therefore the British army took control of Uganda.

In truth this growth of the empire hid the fact that Britain's position in world trade was being overtaken by her rivals. By 1900 Germany was producing more coal and steel than Britain. Industrial innovation was the pride of Germany and the USA, while in Britain the magazine *The Engineer* cautioned that, 'A hasty acceptance of apparent improvements is not to be welcomed'. Britain's rivals were quick to adopt methods of mass production. Their newer factories produced goods more quickly and cheaply than Britain's increasingly old-fashioned workshops and factories.

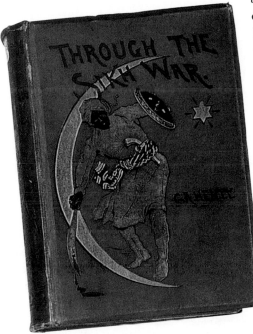

G.A. Henty's books celebrated the British Empire. All his heroes were British boys who fought bravely for their country in titles such as The Young Colonists *and* With Wolfe in Canada *or those shown here. They were enormously popular.*

In South Africa Britain wanted to keep control of the diamond and gold mines, safeguard the trading route round the Cape of Good Hope and maintain her imperial authority at the foot of a continent where British authority had grown so rapidly in the past twenty years. The Boers, the descendants of the Dutch settlers in South Africa, feared, correctly, that the British wanted to take over their two independent states. In 1899 the Boers attacked and the British public expected victory within weeks. Instead the war lasted three years despite a British army of nearly half a million men from various countries in the empire.

The Boers were well-equipped and knew the terrain well. They besieged

British forces in the towns of Kimberley, Ladysmith and Mafeking. Instead of celebrating victories, the British newspapers cheered escapes from defeat. The Boers were finally defeated in 1902, but not before 100,000 Boer civilians had been imprisoned in concentration camps. Disease killed 20,000 of them.

The Boer War showed Britain that she would have to defend her position in the world. Until the 1890s her main imperial rival had been France. Now, under the leadership of Kaiser Wilhelm, Germany appeared the greater threat, rivalling the British and French presence in Africa, China and the Pacific Ocean. Britain's government began to seek allies, beginning with Japan. She no longer felt confident enough to fend off rivals entirely on her own.

Queen Victoria died in 1901. During Victoria's reign Britain had changed more rapidly than at any time in her history, and change was still gathering pace. The latest excitement was the motor car. Yet much remained unaltered. The din that deafened pedestrians in city streets was not the noise of engines, but the rattle of carriage wheels and the pounding of hooves. The air was polluted not by petrol fumes but by fog and smoke from coal fires.

If Daniel Defoe or Josiah Wedgwood had been able to visit Britain in 1901 they would have been surprised, but perhaps not shocked, by what they saw. The twentieth century was to bring far greater change – dramatic, rapid and often terrifying in its effects.

Ludgate Hill in London in 1890. Horse-drawn carriages still thronged the streets, despite the invention of the horseless carriage.

THE ENGLISH ROYAL LINE OF SUCCESSION

❖

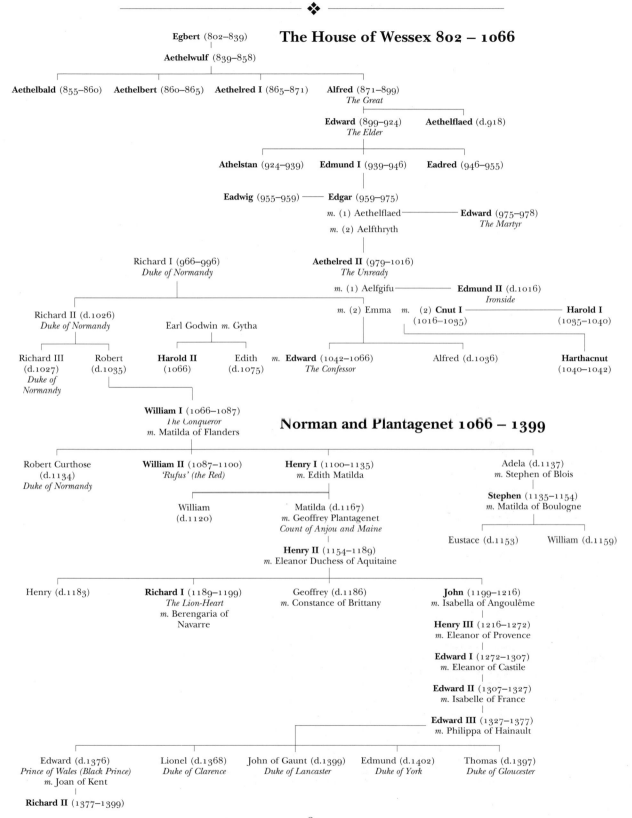

The House of Wessex 802 – 1066

Norman and Plantagenet 1066 – 1399

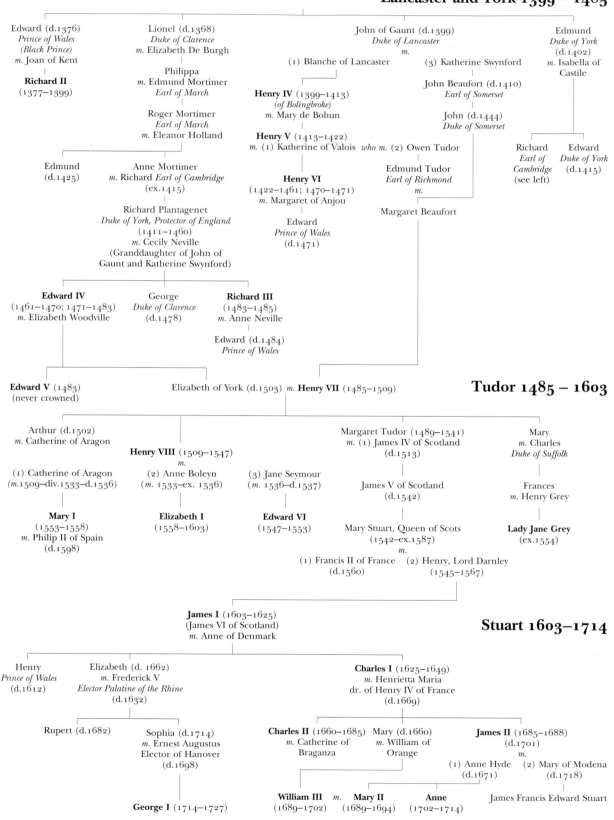

Lancaster and York 1399 – 1485

Tudor 1485 – 1603

Stuart 1603–1714

Hanoverian 1714 – 1901

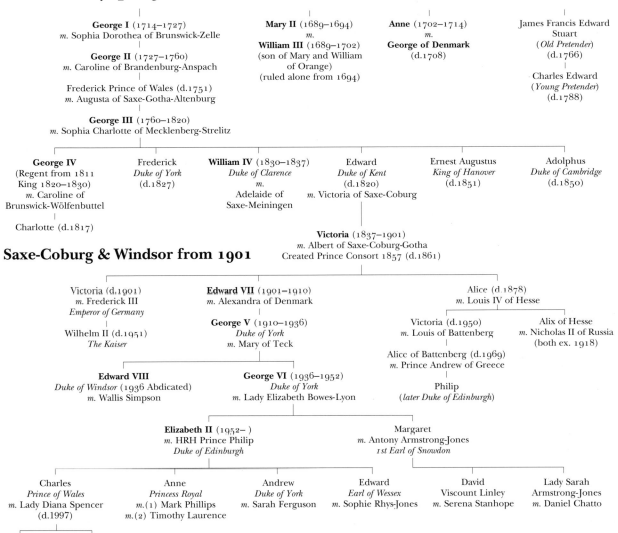

Saxe-Coburg & Windsor from 1901

KINGS AND QUEENS OF SCOTLAND

❖

MAC ALPINE

843–58	Kenneth I
858–62	Donald I
862–77	Constantine I
877–78	Aedh
878–89	Eocha
889–900	Donald II
900–43	Constantine II
943–54	Malcolm I
954–62	Indulf
962–66	Duff
966–71	Colin
971–95	Kenneth II
995–97	Constantine III
997–1005	Kenneth III
1005–34	Malcolm II
1034–40	Duncan I
1040–57	Macbeth
1058	Luiach

CANMORE

1057–93	Malcolm III
1093	Donald Bane
1094	Duncan II
1094–97	Donald Bane
1097–1107	Edgar
1107–24	Alexander I
1124–53	David I
1153–65	Malcolm IV
1165–1214	William I
1214–49	Alexander II
1249–86	Alexander III
1286–90	Margaret
1290–92	No king

BALLIOL

1292–96	John Balliol
1296–1306	No king

BRUCE

1306–29	Robert I
1329–71	David II

STUART

1371–90	Robert II
1390–1406	Robert III
1406–19	Regent Albany
1419–24	Regent Murdoch
1424–37	James I
1437–60	James II
1460–88	James III
1488–1513	James IV
1513–42	James V
1542–67	Mary
1567–1625	JamesVI

In 1603 James VI became King of England, Wales and Ireland. From 1603 onwards the rulers of Scotland are the same as the rulers of England and Wales.

PRIME MINISTERS 1721–2001

❖

1721	Sir Robert Walpole
1741	Earl of Wilmington
1743	Henry Pelham
1754	Duke of Newcastle
1756	Duke of Devonshire
1757	Duke of Newcastle
1762	Earl of Bute
1763	George Grenville
1765	Marquess of Rockingham
1766	Earl of Chatham
1768	Duke of Grafton
1770	Lord North
1782	Marquess of Rockingham
1782	Earl of Shelburne
1783	Duke of Portland
1783	William Pitt
1801	Henry Addington
1804	William Pitt
1806	William Wyndham Grenville
1807	Duke of Portland
1809	Spencer Perceval
1812	Earl of Liverpool
1827	George Canning
1827	Viscount Goderich
1828	Duke of Wellington
1830	Earl Grey
1834	Viscount Melbourne
1834	Duke of Wellington
1834	Sir Robert Peel
1835	Viscount Melbourne
1841	Sir Robert Peel
1846	Lord John Russell
1852	Earl of Derby
1852	Earl of Aberdeen
1855	Viscount Palmerston
1858	Earl of Derby
1859	Viscount Palmerston
1865	Earl Russell
1866	Earl of Derby
1868	Benjamin Disraeli
1868	William Ewart Gladstone
1874	Benjamin Disraeli
1880	William Ewart Gladstone
1885	Marquess of Salisbury
1886	William Ewart Gladstone
1886	Marquess of Salisbury
1892	William Ewart Gladstone
1894	Earl of Rosebery
1895	Marquess of Salisbury
1902	Arthur James Balfour
1905	Sir Henry Campbell-Bannerman
1908	Herbert Henry Asquith
1916	David Lloyd George
1922	Andrew Bonar Law
1923	Stanley Baldwin
1924	James Ramsay MacDonald
1924	Stanley Baldwin
1929	James Ramsay MacDonald
1935	Stanley Baldwin
1937	Neville Chamberlain
1940	Winston Churchill
1945	Clement Attlee
1951	Winston Churchill
1955	Sir Anthony Eden
1957	Harold Macmillan
1963	Sir Alec Douglas-Home
1964	Harold Wilson
1970	Edward Heath
1974	Harold Wilson
1976	James Callaghan
1979	Margaret Thatcher
1990	John Major
1997	Tony Blair

INDEX

ACKNOWLEDGEMENTS

p5 Royal Holloway & Bedford New College/ Bridgeman; p6-7b Mary Evans Picture Library; p7b V & A; p8t Fotomas, bc Wilberforce House, Hull; p8bc Nat. Museums & Galleries on Merseyside (Walker Art Gallery); p9 NPG; p10 Michael Holford; p11t & b Wedgwood Museum; p12b ET; p13t Mansell, c Glasgow Museums: Museum of Transport; p14 ET; p15 Ipswich Museums & Galleries; pp16 Private Collection/ Bridgeman; p17 Private Collection/Bridgeman; p19 V & A; p20t Fotomas; p20-1b Victoria Art Gallery, Bath; p21t Bridgeman; pp 22-3 Harewood House Trust; p24 Mary Evans; p25 Mansell; p26 Nat. Gallery of Canada; p27t King Street Galleries, London/Bridgeman, b ET; p28t Nat. Army Museum, London, b Fotomas; p29 Mansell; p30 ET; p31 Leeds Museums & Galleries; p32 Mansell; pp 33, 34 NPG; p36 Mansell; p37 ET; p38 Nat. Maritime Museum, London/Bridgeman; p40 NG/Bridgeman;

p41t ET, b Bridgeman; p43 Nat. Museums & Galleries of Wales; p44t Science & Society; p44bl Nat. Museum & Galleries on Merseyside/Walker Art Gallery; p44-5b NG; p45t Rural History Centre, Reading, c Bridgeman, br Mansell; p46t Rawtenstall Civic Society; pp46b, 47 Mansell; p48 Rural History Centre, Reading; pp49b, 50 ET; p51 Wedgwood Museum, p52 ET; p53 John Frost Historical Newspapers; p54 Hulton; p55 ET; p56 NPG; p57 Mansell; p58-9b Nat. Gallery of Ireland; pp59t, 61 ET; pp62t & b, 64cl Michael Holford; p63, 64-5b Science & Society Photo Library; p65t AA Photo Library; p66 Bridgeman; p67t Fotomas, b Newport Museum & Art Gallery; p68cl Ann Ronan; p69 Mansell; p70c Royal Archives, Windsor Castle © HM The Queen; p71t Robert Fenton; p72t Mary Evans, b Green Howards Museum; p74tl Science & Society; p74-5t Royal Collection © HM The Queen; p75b Mansell; p76 Trades Union Congress,

London/Bridgeman; p77 Royal Collection © HM The Queen; p78 Robert Opie; p79t Mary Evans, c Marks & Spencer plc; p80l Hulton, r NPG; p81 Tim Smith; p82 Mathew Dawson; pp82-3b, 83t John Gorman; p84 Stapleton Collection/Bridgeman; p85 Ancient Art & Architecture Collection; p86 Green Studio; p87 BL; p88 Hulton;

All maps are by Hardlines, Charlbury, Oxfordshire.

Abbreviations:

BL = British Library; BM = British Museum; CCC = Corpus Christi College; EH = English Heritage; ET = E. T. Archive; IWM = Imperial War Museum; NG = National Gallery, London; NPG = National Portrait Gallery, London; V & A = Victoria & Albert Museum, London; W & N = Weidenfeld & Nicolson Archives